pocket posh® christmas
logic 2

100 PUZZLES

The Puzzle Society™
puzzlesociety.com

Andrews McMeel
Publishing, LLC
Kansas City • Sydney • London

POCKET POSH® CHRISTMAS LOGIC 2

Andrews McMeel Publishing, LLC
an Andrews McMeel Universal company
1130 Walnut Street, Kansas City, Missouri 64106

www.andrewsmcmeel.com
www.puzzlesociety.com

11 12 13 14 15 LEO10 9 8 7 6 5 4 3 2 1

ISBN: 978-1-4494-0898-5

Illustration by Rob and Bob Studio.com

Puzzles supplied under license from Arcturus Publishing.

ATTENTION: SCHOOLS AND BUSINESSES
Andrews McMeel books are available at quantity
discounts with bulk purchase for educational, business, or
sales promotional use. For information, please e-mail the
Andrews McMeel Publishing Special Sales Department:
specialsales@amuniversal.com

how to solve a logic puzzle

Never tried a logic puzzle before? Don't worry! It's really not that hard. All you need is patience and a methodical approach to sort out the positive (yes) and negative (no) information you are given. All the relevant facts are there on the page in front of you.

Let's take things step by step. To make identification easier for beginners, we've lettered the squares of the grid in this example.

	Surname			Hair		
	Dale	Hill	Lake	Black	Brown	Red
Amy	A	B	C	D	E	F
Bill	G	H	I	J	K	L
Colin	M	N	O	P	Q	R
Black	S	T	U			
Brown	V	W	X			
Red	Y	Z	Ω			

Three children each have different surnames and different hair colors. Which is which?

1. The redhead surnamed Dale isn't Bill.

2. Colin (whose hair is brown) isn't the child surnamed Lake.

Child	Surname	Hair

Now start filling in the grid, using ✗s for the "no" (negative) and ✓s for the "yes" (positive) information given in the clues.

Clue 1 states that the redhead is surnamed Dale, so put a ✓ in square Y and ✗s in squares S, V, Z, and Ω. Clue 1 also states that Bill isn't the redhead, so put an ✗ in square L. Thus since Bill isn't surnamed Dale, put an ✗ in square G. Your grid now looks like this:

	Surname			Hair		
	Dale	Hill	Lake	Black	Brown	Red
Amy						
Bill	✗					✗
Colin						
Black	✗					
Brown	✗					
Red	✓	✗	✗			

Clue 2 states that Colin has brown hair, so put a ✓ in square Q and ✗s in squares P, R, E, and K. Your grid now looks like this:

	Surname			Hair		
	Dale	Hill	Lake	Black	Brown	Red
Amy					✗	
Bill	✗				✗	✗
Colin				✗	✓	✗
Black	✗					
Brown	✗					
Red	✓	✗	✗			

Since there are ✗s in both squares K and L, the only possibility remaining for Bill's hair color is black; so you can put a ✓ into square J and an ✗ in square D.

The child with red hair is thus Amy, so put a ✓ in square F. Since the red-haired child is surnamed Dale (clue 1), you can put a ✓ in square A and ✗s in squares B, C, and M.

The child surnamed Lake isn't Colin (clue 2), so Bill; thus you can put a ✓ in square I and ✗s in squares H and O. Since Colin has brown hair, you can put an ✗ in square X and thus a ✓ in W. The child surnamed Hill is thus Colin, so put a ✓ in square N.

Now you can fill the solution box with the details.

Your finished grid and solution box now look like this:

	Surname			Hair		
	Dale	Hill	Lake	Black	Brown	Red
Amy	✓	✗	✗	✗	✗	✓
Bill	✗	✗	✓	✓	✗	✗
Colin	✗	✓	✗	✗	✓	✗
Black	✗	✗	✓			
Brown	✗	✓	✗			
Red	✓	✗	✗			

Child	Surname	Hair
Amy	Dale	Red
Bill	Lake	Black
Colin	Hill	Brown

pocket posh® christmas
logic 2

100 PUZZLES

Lots of Love

Just for fun, four young men sent their girlfriends more than one card on St. Valentine's Day. When questioned, each woman refused to say how many she'd received, thinking it might cause problems! To whom did each man send the cards, how old is she, and how many cards did she receive?

1. Keith's girlfriend is one year older than Fran, whose boyfriend isn't Arthur.

2. George's girlfriend received two fewer cards than were sent to the nineteen-year-old.

3. Debbie received two more cards than Claire, who is one year older than Debbie.

4. Glenda is the youngest of the four women. She didn't receive the highest number of cards.

5. Johnnie sent fewer cards than Arthur.

	Girlfriend				Age				Cards			
	Claire	Debbie	Fran	Glenda	17	18	19	20	6	8	10	12
Arthur												
George												
Johnnie												
Keith												
6 cards												
8 cards												
10 cards												
12 cards												
17 years old												
18 years old												
19 years old												
20 years old												

Boyfriend	Girlfriend	Age	Cards

Home Sweet Home

Five women live in the houses shown on the map below. Each woman's first name, surname, and the name of the street on which she lives start with three different letters of the alphabet. Can you discover every woman's full name, and address?

1. Ms. Vanderbilt lives further east than Heidi.

2. Veronica Roberts lives further east than Angela.

3. Ms. Aston lives further east than Laura.

4. Rachel lives further south than Ms. Holt.

	Surname					Address				
	Aston	Holt	Lever	Roberts	Vanderbilt	Apple Ave.	High Hill	Low Lane	Rail Road	Vale View
Angela										
Heidi										
Laura										
Rachel										
Veronica										
Apple Ave.					
High Hill					
Low Lane					
Rail Road					
Vale View					

High Hill   Low Lane

Vale View   Rail Road

Apple Avenue

Woman	Surname	Address

Wrecked!

Five cars each had an accident in the small town of Windy Ridge last week. No one was hurt but each car was so badly damaged as to be considered a wreck. The local garage has towed away the vehicles and lined them up as you see on the plan below. What did each vehicle hit, and on which street?

1. The car that ran into the back of a truck is further right than the one collected from Maple Road.

2. The car that suffered damage (but not as a result of hitting a wall) on Edge Avenue is between two others: that collected from Oxford Street and the one that went into the side of a stationary bus.

3. The car that hit a tree is further right than (but not next to) the one collected from Forest Road.

4. The car that had a collision on Sycamore Drive is further left than (but not next to) the one that hit a wall.

	Bus	Traffic sign	Tree	Truck	Wall	Edge Avenue	Forest Road	Maple Road	Oxford Street	Sycamore Drive
Car A										
Car B										
Car C										
Car D										
Car E										
Edge Avenue										
Forest Road										
Maple Road										
Oxford Street										
Sycamore Drive										

LEFT ⇐   RIGHT ⇒

A   B   C   D   E

Car	Hit	Street

Supper Party

Donna hosted a Supperware party last night and invited all of her friends, four of whom decided to surprise her by contributing items of food for people to share. In what order did the four arrive, what did she bring and how much did she spend on her order of goods for sale at the party?

1. Kathy spent five dollars more than (and arrived immediately after) the woman who baked a large chocolate cake for the event.

2. Stella (who made a batch of cookies) spent more than the woman who was last to arrive, but not ten dollars more.

3. The woman who made doughnuts spent less than Natalie, who arrived fifth.

	Arrival				Made				Spent			
	Fifth	Seventh	Eighth	Ninth	Cake	Cookies	Doughnuts	Scones	$25	$30	$35	$40
Kathy												
Natalie												
Pam												
Stella												
$25									
$30									
$35									
$40									
Cake					
Cookies					
Doughnuts					
Scones					

Friend	Arrival	Made	Spent

Traveling Home

After an afternoon spent shopping in town, four friends made their way to the bus station in order to catch a bus home. Each lives in a different area, so took a different bus home than the other three. Can you work out the name of the area where each lives, the number of his or her bus, and the time it departed?

1. Helen doesn't live in the Lakeside or Wood Lodge areas of town.

2. The bus to Lakeside has a lower number than the one which departed at 5:08 p.m.

3. Micky's home is in The Moorings. His bus departed immediately before that taken by Sue. Sue didn't board the No. 87 bus.

4. The bus to Amber Hill left later than the one taken by Andrew.

5. Andrew's bus left later than the No. 16.

	Area				Bus No.				Departed			
	Amber Hill	Lakeside	The Moorings	Wood Lodge	16	24	42	87	5:05 P.M.	5:08 P.M.	5:12 P.M.	5:15 P.M.
Andrew												
Helen												
Micky												
Sue												
5:05 P.M.												
5:08 P.M.												
5:12 P.M.												
5:15 P.M.												
No. 16												
No. 24												
No. 42												
No. 87												

Friend	Area	Bus No.	Departed

Birthday Presents

Lynda received five presents on her birthday, one from each member of her family. Can you work through the clues to decide what each person gave, and the order in which it was opened?

1. Lynda opened the present from her brother earlier than the one from her sister, but later than the parcel that contained the fluffy teddy bear.

2. The wristwatch was a present from her father.

3. Her grandmother's gift of a book of fairy stories was opened immediately after the present Lynda received from her mother, which wasn't the first she opened.

4. The final present Lynda opened contained a doll she had wanted for a very long time!

	Present					Order				
	Book	Doll	Kite	Teddy bear	Watch	First	Second	Third	Fourth	Fifth
Brother										
Father										
Grandma										
Mother										
Sister										
First					
Second					
Third					
Fourth					
Fifth					

Giver	Present	Order

Cover Story

The diagram below shows five books on a shelf. Each has a cover of a different color and is on a different subject. As you can see from the diagram, the books are of two different heights (A and D being taller than B, C, and E). Can you discover the color of each book's cover, as well as its subject?

1. The book with a blue cover is touching both the one with a yellow cover and the book on art (which is taller than that with a yellow cover).

2. The illustrated book of wild flowers is next to and left of the book with a green cover.

3. The book on fishing has a red cover and is shorter than (and not directly next to) the book on sport.

	Color					Subject				
	Blue	Brown	Green	Red	Yellow	Art	Birds	Fishing	Sport	Wild flowers
Book A										
Book B										
Book C										
Book D										
Book E										
Art										
Birds										
Fishing										
Sport										
Wild flowers										

LEFT ⇐   RIGHT ⇒

A B C D E

Book	Color	Subject

Island Weddings

Each of the four couples who have kindly agreed to appear in this puzzle got married on different islands last year. The clues below will link the details of each bride and groom together with the place and month in which they were married.

1. No bride or groom married in a month that starts with the same letter as that of his or her name; and no bride married a groom with a name that starts with the same letter as that of her own.

2. Julia and her husband Carl married earlier in the year than the couple whose wedding took place in Tenerife.

3. The wedding in Barbados took place three months before Danny's marriage, but later than the wedding on the island of Sardinia.

4. The bride who married in Majorca isn't Sarah.

	Carl	Danny	Mike	Stuart	Barbados	Majorca	Sardinia	Tenerife	March	June	September	December
Deirdre												
Julia												
Maria												
Sarah												
March												
June												
September												
December												
Barbados												
Majorca												
Sardinia												
Tenerife												

Bride	Groom	Island	Month

Nieces and Nephews

Four friends each have different numbers of nieces and nephews. Can you discover each man's full name, and the number of nieces and nephews he has?

1. Patrick has one more niece than nephew. Mr. Venner has more nephews than nieces.

2. Mr. Harte has the same number of nieces as his friend Ronnie has nephews. Ronnie's surname isn't Thorpe.

3. Norman has two more nieces than nephews.

4. The man with nine nieces and six nephews isn't Mr. Grainger.

	Surname				Nieces				Nephews			
	Grainger	Harte	Thorpe	Venner	6	7	8	9	5	6	7	8
Norman												
Patrick												
Ronnie												
Theo												
5 nephews												
6 nephews												
7 nephews												
8 nephews												
6 nieces												
7 nieces												
8 nieces												
9 nieces												

Friend	Surname	Nieces	Nephews

Snowballs

Five little boys were delighted when the snow fell last weekend and they all went out to play together, each dressed up against the cold. Their mothers told them to take care, but boys will be boys . . . and each hit something he shouldn't. Discover the color of each boy's hat, as well as what he hit with one of his snowballs.

1. The boy who hit the cyclist (causing her to wobble precariously!) wore a bright red hat, so was easily identified!

2. Simon (whose hat is blue) wasn't the boy who got shouted at by a neighbor after hitting him on the back with a snowball.

3. The boy in the green hat inadvertently hit a dog in a nearby garden. Larry's hat isn't green.

4. Martin's very first snowball hit the side of a passing car.

5. William wore the purple hat.

	Blue	Cream	Green	Purple	Red	Car	Cyclist	Dog	Neighbor	Window
Andy										
Larry										
Martin										
Simon										
William										
Car										
Cyclist										
Dog										
Neighbor										
Window										

Boy	Hat	Hit

Joint Efforts

The latest album by the band Moods features five tracks jointly written by two of its members (one person setting words to music written by another person). Who wrote the words and music for each of the listed tracks?

1. Ben wrote the music for "Single Girl" and James wrote the words for "Stay Free".

2. The song for which Suzi wrote the music and Tania supplied the words isn't "Why Not?", nor did Will have any part in the composition of "Why Not?".

3. Tania wrote the music for "No Thoughts".

4. Ben didn't supply the words to the music composed by James.

	Words					Music				
	Ben	James	Suzi	Tania	Will	Ben	James	Suzi	Tania	Will
"Fast Mover"										
"No Thoughts"										
"Single Girl"										
"Stay Free"										
"Why Not?"										
Ben										
James										
Suzi										
Tania										
Will										

Track	Words	Music

The Name Game

The diagram below shows four film actors, who are about to take part in a television game show. Can you identify each man by his stage name, real name, and the title of the latest film in which he starred?

1. The man known to the public as Arthur Ayr is sitting directly next to and between Kevin Marsh and the star of *The Pirate*.

2. Kevin Marsh is further right than the man who calls himself Clarke Crowe. Neither man is the star of *Wise Choice*.

3. Liam Pearce's stage name is Dave Darnley. He is sitting further right than Tom Watson.

4. Neither man B nor man C has played a role in *Fortunate*.

	Stage Name				Real Name				Film			
	Arthur Ayr	Bill Benson	Clark Crowe	Dave Darnley	Bert Cox	Kevin Marsh	Liam Pearce	Tom Watson	Dead Calm	Fortunate	The Pirate	Wise Choice
Man A												
Man B												
Man C												
Man D												
Dead Calm												
Fortunate												
The Pirate												
Wise Choice												
Bert Cox												
Kevin Marsh												
Liam Pearce												
Tom Watson												

5. The star of *Dead Calm* is sitting further left than the man most widely known as Bill Benson.

LEFT ⇐   RIGHT ⇒

A B C D

Man	Stage	Real	Film

Resolutions

Knowing that if they made New Year's resolutions, they probably wouldn't keep them, the four members of the Johnson family played a game of three rounds, using the letters of the word RESOLUTION. In the first round they had to find a word of three letters, the second a word of four letters, and the third a word of five letters. Which words did each player make?

1. Adam's three-letter word started with the same letter as the five-letter word made by the player whose four-letter word was ROSE.

2. Lorna didn't use the letter "T" in any word she made. The player whose four-letter word was TILE didn't use the letter "R" in any word.

3. Jill's three-letter word began with the same letter as her five-letter word.

4. Pete's five-letter word started with an earlier letter of the alphabet than his three-letter word.

5. Adam wasn't the player who made the word STONE.

	3 Letters				4 Letters				5 Letters			
	LIT	NOT	ORE	SIN	LOSE	NOTE	ROSE	TILE	LOUSE	OUTER	ROUSE	STONE
Adam												
Jill												
Lorna												
Pete												
LOUSE												
OUTER												
ROUSE												
STONE												
LOSE												
NOTE												
ROSE												
TILE												

Player	3 Letters	4 Letters	5 Letters

New Teachers

Four new teachers joined the staff at the local school at the beginning of the year, all of whom had been employed in other jobs before realizing that their true vocation was teaching. Can you discover each person's previous line of employment and the subject he or she now teaches at the school?

1. Not surprisingly, the former musician (with a rock band) now teaches music at the school. Mrs. Elliott's subject isn't music.

2. Mr. Farmer teaches geography and has never worked as a clerk.

3. The one-time circus acrobat now teaches biology, unlike Miss Cross, who isn't teaching music or English at the school.

4. Mr. Gould was once a computer hardware salesperson.

	Former Job					Subject				
	Acrobat	Bar manager	Clerk	Musician	Salesperson	Biology	English	Geography	History	Music
Miss Cross										
Mr. Dawson										
Mrs. Elliott										
Mr. Farmer										
Mr. Gould										
Biology										
English										
Geography										
History										
Music										

Teacher	Former Job	Subject

Birthdays

Coincidentally, five friends all have birthdays on the first of the month, although in different months. None has a surname that begins with the same letter as that of his or her first name and none has a birthday in a month that begins with the same letter as his or her first name or surname. What is each friend's full name and in which month is his or her birthday?

1. Jenny's birthday is either the month before or the month after that of the person surnamed Allen.

2. Arnold's birthday is earlier in the year than that of the person surnamed Major.

3. Stephen's birthday is either two months before or two months after that of the person surnamed Jones.

4. Marjorie Oldman is the tallest of the five friends.

	Allen	Jones	Major	Oldman	Saunders	April	May	July	September	October
Arnold										
Jenny										
Marjorie										
Owen										
Stephen										
April										
May										
July										
September										
October										

Forename	Surname	Month

Readers

Four people who called in at the public library this morning each spent a few hours in the reference section, studying various books on a particular subject. At what time did each arrive, for how long did he or she stay, and what was the subject of interest to each reader?

1. The person interested in butterflies arrived thirty minutes earlier than the person who was keen to gain more knowledge on the history of flags.

2. Judy studied several books on coins and stayed in the library for one hour longer than the person interested in politics, who arrived later than Judy.

3. Lionel stayed in the library for half an hour longer than Trish who, in turn, stayed in the library for longer than the person who arrived at 9:00 a.m.

	Arrived				Stayed				Studied			
	8:45 A.M.	9:00 A.M.	9:15 A.M.	9:30 A.M.	2½ hours	3 hours	3½ hours	4 hours	Butterflies	Coins	Flags	Politics
Judy												
Lionel												
Martin												
Trish												
Butterflies												
Coins												
Flags												
Politics												
2½ hours												
3 hours												
3½ hours												
4 hours												

Reader	Arrived	Stayed	Studied

Winter Snowsports

Each year, the town of Mountvale plays host to a winter snowsports competition, the finals of four sports being held on different days at different locations nearby. Using the clues and the map should help you to decide not only the location at which each event took place, but also the name of the man who won each of the men's events, and the day on which it took place.

1. Monday's event took place at a location further south than that at which Max won his event (not the snowboarding contest, which was held to the east of Mountvale).

2. The snowboarding contest was held later in the week than the event won by Anton, but earlier in the week than the day of the skating competition.

3. Thursday's event was won by Wilhelm and took place at a location further south than the site of the ski jumping contest, which took place later in the week than the toboggan race.

4. The snowboard event was held the day before the event at site D.

	Location				Winner				Day			
	A	B	C	D	Anton	George	Max	Wilhelm	Monday	Tuesday	Wednesday	Thursday
Skating												
Ski jump												
Snowboard												
Toboggan												
Monday								
Tuesday								
Wednesday								
Thursday								
Anton				
George				
Max				
Wilhelm				

N W E S

A D Mountvale B C

Event	Location	Winner	Day

Dividing the Spoils

After his own vessel had been sunk by a Spanish warship, Captain Rook decided to retire and share what they could salvage from the wreck amongst the five surviving members of his motley crew. Every man took a share of the doubloons and ducats according to his time with Captain Rook—and Captain Rook made off with all the rest: jewels, guineas, and pieces of eight! What was each man's share?

1. Dirty Dave got thirty more ducats than doubloons and ten more ducats than the man who received the largest quantity of doubloons.

2. Horrible Hugh didn't receive the highest or lowest quantities of either doubloons or ducats, but he did get more doubloons than Nasty Ned, and fewer ducats than Sly Sam.

3. Sly Sam got fewer doubloons (but thirty more ducats) than Nasty Ned.

	Doubloons					Ducats				
	120	130	140	150	160	120	140	150	160	170
Dirty Dave										
Evil Edmund										
Horrible Hugh										
Nasty Ned										
Sly Sam										
120 ducats										
140 ducats										
150 ducats										
160 ducats										
170 ducats										

Pirate	Doubloons	Ducats

Boating on the Lake

Five yachts were on Great Pine Lake this morning, at the time the aerial view below was drawn. Each was traveling in a clockwise direction. Can you identify each yacht according to its name and the color of its sails? (Note—The reference in the clues to "looking around the lake in a clockwise direction" does not necessarily mean starting with yacht A.)

1. Looking around the lake in a clockwise direction, we can see: *Tamarind*; the yacht with white sails; another yacht; *West Wind*; and the yacht with orange sails, which isn't in position B on the plan.

2. Looking around the lake in a clockwise direction, we can see: *Skipper*; the yacht with the yellow sails; *Ariadne*; another yacht; and the yacht with red sails, which isn't in position D on the plan.

3. *Lena May* has turquoise sails and is neither in position B nor in position D on the plan below.

	Name					Sails				
	Ariadne	Lena May	Skipper	Tamarind	West Wind	Orange	Red	Turquoise	White	Yellow
Yacht A										
Yacht B										
Yacht C										
Yacht D										
Yacht E										
Orange										
Red										
Turquoise										
White										
Yellow										

Clockwise

A
X

E
X

B
X

D
X

C
X

Yacht	Name	Sails

Sports Car Racers

The annual Wheelsville Sports Car race took place last weekend. Can you discover the full name of each driver who finished in the first four, the car he drove, and his final position in the race?

1. Terry's car finished one place ahead of the Porsche, which wasn't driven by Mr. Bishop. Terry's surname is neither Bishop nor Davis.

2. Mr. Bishop's car finished more than one place behind the Mercedes.

3. The Jaguar finished more than one place ahead of the car driven by Mr. Davis. Benjamin (who didn't drive the Jaguar) wasn't second in the race and isn't surnamed Davis.

4. Harry's car finished one place ahead of the Ferrari.

5. Keith's surname isn't Exbury.

	Bishop	Colt	Davis	Exbury	Ferrari	Jaguar	Mercedes	Porsche	First	Second	Third	Fourth
Benjamin												
Harry												
Keith												
Terry												
First												
Second												
Third												
Fourth												
Ferrari												
Jaguar												
Mercedes												
Porsche												

Driver	Surname	Car	Position

Romantic Women

The annual Cupid Prize for Romantic Fiction has been won by four different women over the past few years. For each of the years listed in the grid below, can you discover the title of the winning novel, together with the pen name of the writer of the story?

1. *True Devotion* won the Cupid Prize the year after the novel written by Ms. Dale.

2. Lara's novel won the prize the year before that written by Amelia, but the year after *Sad Souls*.

3. Ms. Hart, who penned *No Return*, took the Cupid Prize two years after *Bella's Tale* had won.

4. Maggie's surname is Maughan.

	Bella's Tale	No Return	Sad Souls	True Devotion	Amelia	Lara	Maggie	Sheila	Bennett	Dale	Hart	Maughan
2004												
2005												
2006												
2007												
Bennett												
Dale												
Hart												
Maughan												
Amelia												
Lara												
Maggie												
Sheila												

Year	Title	First Name	Surname

Endurance Trial

The National Television Company is currently running a series of programs where viewers can raise money for charity by sponsoring celebrities who participate in an endurance trial. On which day last week did each person appear and what trial did he or she undergo to raise money for charity?

1. The trial that involved climbing a steep hill while carrying a full backpack took place the day after that on which a well-known supermodel had agreed to sit suspended above a pit of ferocious-looking (but harmless) snakes.

2. The hockey player who appeared on Monday's program wasn't the person who ate a plate of wriggling grubs.

3. The celebrity who sat in an icy bath appeared the day after the comedian.

4. The magician took part in the program the day before the singer did so.

	Day					Trial				
	Monday	Tuesday	Wednesday	Thursday	Friday	Climbing	Grub-eating	Icy bath	Snake pit	Tank of eels
Comedian										
Hockey player										
Magician										
Singer										
Supermodel										
Climbing					
Grub-eating					
Icy bath					
Snake pit					
Tank of eels					

Celebrity	Day	Trial

Construction

Five commuters who take different routes to work were stuck in traffic jams this morning, due to construction. Can you decide who was held up by each of the listed companies and for how long?

1. The telephone company was responsible for the construction that caused one commuter to be delayed for four minutes longer than the person whose delay was caused by the gas company.

2. Mrs. Barton was delayed for two minutes longer than Mr. King, but not as a result of works being carried out by either the gas or line painting companies.

3. Mr. Walters was delayed for six minutes longer than the commuter who had to wait in a queue caused by the electricity company's construction (which didn't affect Mrs. Barton).

4. Mr. Price's delay was longer than that of Miss Scott, which, in turn, was longer than that of at least one other commuter.

	Commuter					Time				
	Mrs. Barton	Mr. King	Mr. Price	Miss Scott	Mr. Walters	10 minutes	12 minutes	14 minutes	16 minutes	18 minutes
Electricity										
Gas										
Line painting										
Telephone										
Water										
10 minutes										
12 minutes										
14 minutes										
16 minutes										
18 minutes										

Company	Commuter	Time

Market Regulars

The town of Burnside has a market four days per week and stall No. 1 is used on the different days by four different traders. Can you match the traders to the day on which he or she works at the market, what he or she sells, and the number of years that he or she has been trading?

1. Ken uses stall No. 1 either two days before or two days after the person who has been trading for the longest time.

2. Sally works at the market later in the week than the person who sells fruit.

3. Vincent works at the market on Fridays and has been trading for half as many years as the bookseller.

4. Jane uses stall No. 1 later in the week than the person who has traded for eight years, but earlier in the week than the person who sells pottery.

5. Sally has been trading for fewer years than Ken.

	Day				Goods				Years			
	Monday	Tuesday	Wednesday	Friday	Books	Fruit	Flowers	Pottery	4	5	8	10
Jane												
Ken												
Sally												
Vincent												
4 years												
5 years												
8 years												
10 years												
Books												
Fruit												
Flowers												
Pottery												

Trader	Day	Goods	Years

Playing Cards

The four men in this puzzle are playing a game of cards and each has three in his hand: one club, one heart and one spade. Can you discover which three cards are in each man's hand? (Note—A = ace, J = jack, Q = queen, and K = king; and in the game ace = 1, jack = 11, queen = 12, king = 13, and the values of the other cards are as per their numbers.)

1. The man with the seven of hearts has a club with the same value as that of the spade in Henry's hand and a spade with a higher value than Henry's.

2. The man with the queen of clubs is holding a spade with a value two lower than that of Damian's spade.

3. Simon's spade has a higher value than that of his club (which has a higher value than George's club).

4. Damian's club has a lower value than that of his spade.

	Club				Heart				Spade			
	3	5	7	Q	4	7	9	K	A	3	5	J
Damian												
George												
Henry												
Simon												
Spade A												
Spade 3												
Spade 5												
Spade J												
Heart 4												
Heart 7												
Heart 9												
Heart K												

5. Simon's heart has a lower value than that of his club.

6. Henry's heart has a higher value than George's heart.

Player	Club	Heart	Spade

Mother's Taxi

Louise leads a busy life during the week, driving her children to and from school and the various clubs they attend in the evenings. Can you decide the club each child belongs to and the evening of the week that it meets?

1. The guitar club meets earlier in the week than the swimming club, which meets the evening before the club Darren attends.

2. Lisa's club meets earlier in the week than the drama club, which meets earlier in the week than the club William attends.

3. The bird-watching club meets earlier in the week than the club of which Poppy is a member, which meets earlier in the week than the club Bob attends.

4. The table tennis club meets either the evening before or the evening after the club Bob attends.

	Bird-watching	Drama	Guitar	Swimming	Table tennis	Monday	Tuesday	Wednesday	Thursday	Friday
		Club					Evening			
Bob										
Darren										
Lisa										
Poppy										
William										
Monday										
Tuesday										
Wednesday										
Thursday										
Friday										

Child	Club	Evening

Split Personalities

Fed up with having to study Shakespeare at school, Jonathon has cut pictures of five Shakespearean characters each into three pieces (head, body, and legs) and then reassembled them in such a way that each "new" picture contains pieces of three "old" ones. How have the pictures been reassembled?

1. Banquo's legs are now attached to Othello's body, which isn't topped by Juliet's head.

2. Romeo's head is now in the same picture as Juliet's body.

3. Othello's head and Juliet's legs are in two different pictures.

4. Romeo's body is in the same picture as Desdemona's legs, which are in a different picture than Juliet's head.

	Body					Legs				
	Banquo	Desdemona	Juliet	Othello	Romeo	Banquo	Desdemona	Juliet	Othello	Romeo
Head Banquo										
Desdemona										
Juliet										
Othello										
Romeo										
Legs Banquo										
Desdemona										
Juliet										
Othello										
Romeo										

Head	Body	Legs

Exciting News

On four days last week, Ronnie received an exciting piece of news concerning a friend or relative. How did Ronnie get this news on the days listed in the grid below, from whom, and about what?

1. Brenda informed Ronnie of her pregnancy, but not via the e-mail, which Ronnie received the day after hearing of his cousin's university graduation.

2. Matthew wrote the letter, but not about a graduation or a new home.

3. Tuesday's news was told to Ronnie in person, but not by Brenda or Jeff. Nor did Brenda's news come on Friday.

	Method				From				Subject			
	E-mail	In person	Letter	Phone call	Brenda	Jeff	Matthew	Tina	Engagement	Graduation	New home	Pregnancy
Tuesday												
Wednesday												
Thursday												
Friday												
Engagement												
Graduation												
New home												
Pregnancy												
Brenda												
Jeff												
Matthew												
Tina												

Day	Method	From	Subject

Colorful Drawers

In an attempt to cheer herself up by brightening her bedroom, Linda painted the fronts of twelve drawers of the dresser in which she stores her personal effects. She only had four pots of paint: blue, green, red, and yellow, so her room is now very bright indeed. On each of the three levels of drawers, all four colors were used. What is the color of each drawer?

1. Drawer No. 7 is red and is directly next to and left of a drawer of the same color as No. 11.

2. Drawer No. 9 is of the same color as drawer No. 4, which isn't red.

3. The blue drawer in the top row is further left than the blue drawer in the bottom row, but further right than the blue drawer in the middle row.

4. Drawer No. 12 is not of the same color as drawer No. 5.

5. No yellow drawer is directly next to and left of a blue drawer in the top row or the middle row.

		Top				Middle				Bottom		
		1	2	3	4	5	6	7	8	9	10	11	12
Blue													
Green													
Red													
Yellow													

Bottom	9				
	10				
	11				
	12				

Middle	5				
	6				
	7				
	8				

▭ 1	▭ 2	▭ 3	▭ 4
▭ 5	▭ 6	▭ 7	▭ 8
▭ 9	▭ 10	▭ 11	▭ 12

LEFT ⇐   RIGHT ⇒

Color	Top	Middle	Bottom

Island Stamps

Candy collects stamps issued by the five island republics that form Midlonesia. Each is ruled by a president whose face features on the stamps (as well as many other items!), and Candy has been fascinated by Midlonesia politics for as long as she can remember. Can you discover when each president came to power, together with the value of the latest stamp from each country?

1. The stamp carrying a portrait of President Zag has a value of two Midlonesian dollars more than that of the man who came to power four years before President Zeg.

2. President Zog's face features on the stamp with the highest value. He took control of his country's affairs four years after the man whose face appears on the $3 stamps came to power.

3. The man who came to power in 1996 has his picture on a stamp with a value one Midlonesian dollar less than that featuring President Zug, who came to power in 1988.

| | Year | | | | | Value | | | | |
	1988	1990	1994	1996	1998	$2	$3	$4	$5	$6
Zag										
Zeg										
Zig										
Zog										
Zug										
$2					
$3					
$4					
$5					
$6					

President	Year	Value

Appointments to View

Jim and Cora are looking to buy their first home and each weekday last week they visited a different property at a different time of day, although they still haven't seen anything they'd like to buy. At what time was the appointment to view each day, and what fault did Jim and Cora find with the property they saw?

1. The house that the couple thought was too small was visited at a time three quarters of an hour later than Thursday's appointment.

2. On Monday, Jim and Cora dismissed one house as being too noisy because it was next to a very busy road.

3. The 11:30 a.m. appointment was the day after the 10:15 a.m. appointment.

4. The house which they considered to be too isolated was viewed at 12:15 p.m. the day before the one they thought was too cold.

	Time					Problem				
	10:15 A.M.	10:45 A.M.	11:30 A.M.	12:15 P.M.	12:45 P.M.	Too cold	Too damp	Too isolated	Too noisy	Too small
Monday										
Tuesday										
Wednesday										
Thursday										
Friday										
Too cold										
Too damp										
Too isolated										
Too noisy										
Too small										

Day	Time	Problem

TV Favorites

Four women who live in neighboring properties met for coffee yesterday and began to discuss their favorite types of television program. Discover each neighbor's full name, the number of the house at which she lives, and the type of program each prefers to view.

1. Wildlife programs are the preferred viewing of the woman who lives next to and between Mrs. Rigden and Sheila (who isn't Mrs. Vance).

2. Mrs. Derby lives further east than Jean, but further west than the woman whose favorite programs are on the subject of travel.

3. Helen prefers to watch sports to any other program. She lives in a house with a higher number than that of the crime program enthusiast (who isn't Mrs. Vance).

4. Miss Edwards doesn't watch crime programs at all.

	Surname				House No.				Favorite			
	Derby	Edwards	Rigden	Vance	1	2	3	4	Crime	Sports	Travel	Wildlife
Helen												
Jean												
Paula												
Sheila												
Crime													
Sports								
Travel								
Wildlife								
No. 1				
No. 2				
No. 3				
No. 4				

N W E S

| | 1 | 2 | 3 | 4 |

Woman	Surname	House No.	Favorite

Playing Together

The new play at the Central Theatre has just four characters, each played by an amateur thespian. What is the name and description of each character in the play, and what is the full name of the man playing him?

1. In all cases the name and description of the character plus the first name and surname of the man playing him begin with four different letters of the alphabet.

2. Neither Chester nor Mr. Davies (who is taller than Chester) plays the role of Pritchard. Nor does Mr. Davies play the part of the painter.

3. The cop in the play isn't Daly; and neither Daly nor the cop is played by Peter.

4. Bayliss is the town drunkard in the play.

| | Description | | | | Actor | | | | Surname | | | |
	Burglar	Cop	Drunkard	Painter	Bob	Chester	Dave	Peter	Brown	Crouch	Davies	Pryce
Bayliss												
Coren												
Daly												
Pritchard												
Brown												
Crouch												
Davies												
Pryce												
Bob												
Chester												
Dave												
Peter												

Role	Desc.	Actor	Surname

Back to Work

Five people returned to work yesterday, having spent various lengths of time away due to ailments and injuries. Can you discover how long each person had been away from work and for what reason?

1. The person away from work for four days had a sore throat.

2. Mr. Chester was away for three days longer than Miss Bourn.

3. Mrs. Hudson was away for less time than the person with a sprained ankle, but longer than the person who suffered for many days with a stomach bug.

4. Mr. Yates sustained a head injury while aboard a friend's yacht. He wasn't away from work for exactly one day longer than Mr. Newton.

	Absence (days)					Reason				
	4	5	6	8	9	Cough	Head injury	Sore throat	Sprained ankle	Stomach bug
Miss Bourn										
Mr. Chester										
Mrs. Hudson										
Mr. Newton										
Mr. Yates										
Cough										
Head injury										
Sore throat										
Sprained ankle										
Stomach bug										

Name	Absence	Reason

Trading Cards

When Georgina moved into her new house last week, five neighbors kindly left her cards for the services of workmen they could recommend. This morning, Georgina pinned the cards onto her notice board, a diagram of which is shown below. Whose services did each neighbor recommend and what number identifies his card?

1. The card given by Laura is next to and above that of the electrician, which is further right than the one giving details of the plumber.

2. Norah gave Georgina the card showing the gardener's name and telephone number, which is higher on the board than the one given by Cora.

3. The decorator's card is in a position with a number one higher than that of the card which Flora gave to Georgina.

4. The carpenter was recommended by Dora.

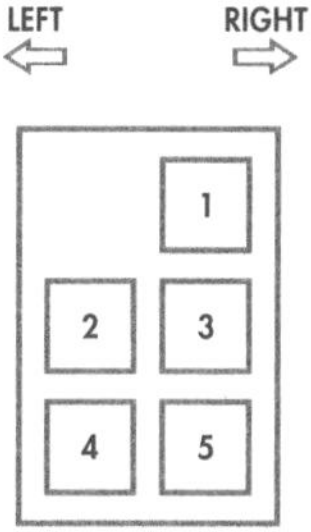

	Tradesman					Card No.				
	Carpenter	Decorator	Electrician	Gardener	Plumber	1	2	3	4	5
Cora										
Dora										
Flora										
Laura										
Norah										
Card 1					
Card 2					
Card 3					
Card 4					
Card 5					

LEFT ⇐ RIGHT ⇒

Board positions: 1 (top right); 2, 3 (middle); 4, 5 (bottom)

Neighbor	Tradesman	Card No.

Cereal Choices

As part of a survey on breakfast cereals, four housewives were asked their preferences from a choice of four leading brands. Each was asked to choose a different cereal in first, second, and third place and (coincidentally) no woman's choices were the same as those of another woman. For instance, one woman's first choice was Munchies, so no one else rated Munchies in first place. In what order did each woman rate the cereals?

1. The woman whose first choice was Flakies rated second the cereal that Julie rated in third place.

2. The woman who chose Chockies second also rated Munchies third. Thelma didn't place Munchies at all in her three choices.

3. Sandy chose Crunchies second. Louisa's second choice wasn't Chockies.

	First				Second				Third			
	Chockies	Crunchies	Flakies	Munchies	Chockies	Crunchies	Flakies	Munchies	Chockies	Crunchies	Flakies	Munchies
Julie												
Louisa												
Sandy												
Thelma												
Third Chockies												
Crunchies												
Flakies												
Munchies												
Second Chockies												
Crunchies												
Flakies												
Munchies												

Name	First	Second	Third

Waiter's Dilemma

The waiter looking after the diners at tables 1–4 was sure he'd remember what was ordered, so didn't bother to write down anything. He managed well for the starters and main courses, but by the time it came to the dessert course, his memory failed and everyone was given something he or she hadn't ordered. At which numbered table did each sit and what did he or she order (and subsequently receive) for the dessert course?

1. Desmond had ordered the strawberry sorbet, but had actually started to eat the dessert put in front of him, before it was taken to the right person!

2. Gina sat at a table with a number one higher than that of the diner who ordered apple pie, but lower than that taken by the customer who received apple pie.

	Table				Ordered				Received			
	1	2	3	4	Apple pie	Cheesecake	Ice cream	Sorbet	Apple pie	Cheesecake	Ice cream	Sorbet
Desmond												
Eileen												
Frederick												
Gina												
Received Apple pie												
Received Cheesecake												
Received Ice cream												
Received Sorbet												
Ordered Apple pie												
Ordered Cheesecake												
Ordered Ice cream												
Ordered Sorbet												

3. The diner who ordered cheesecake sat at a table with a number one lower than that taken by Eileen, who received the chocolate ice cream.

Diner	Table No.	Ordered	Received

Good Deeds

The five Good sisters each do voluntary work for the elderly citizens of the community on one day every week. Each woman undertakes one task in the morning and a different task in the afternoon. Can you discover what each did in these two periods yesterday?

1. The woman who cleaned an elderly person's apartment in the morning also did another citizen's laundry in the afternoon. She isn't Faith, whose morning job was the same as Constance's afternoon job (not laundry).

2. Hope spent yesterday afternoon cooking. Hope's morning job was the same as the task undertaken by Joy in the afternoon.

3. Charity spent the morning gardening in the grounds of a local retirement home.

	Morning					Afternoon				
	Cleaning	Cooking	Gardening	Laundry	Shopping	Cleaning	Cooking	Gardening	Laundry	Shopping
Charity										
Constance										
Faith										
Hope										
Joy										
Cleaning										
Cooking										
Gardening										
Laundry										
Shopping										

Afternoon

Sister	Morning	Afternoon

Passing the Time

Five motorists caught up in an unusually long traffic jam passed the time by engaging in different activities. Can you identify the driver of each vehicle (the two lanes of traffic are as shown on the plan below) and say how he or she spent the time while waiting for the traffic to start moving again?

1. Always prepared for delays, Patricia got out her knitting and continued with the hat she was making. She was, however, rather annoyed when the man in the car alongside her own began to sing at the top of his voice.

2. Beth's car was next to and ahead of that driven by Malcolm, whose car was in a different lane to Richard's vehicle.

3. The occupant of car D spent the time writing a letter.

4. Judy didn't phone anyone during the time she spent in the traffic jam.

	Beth	Judy	Malcolm	Patricia	Richard	Knitting	Phoning	Reading	Singing	Writing
Car A										
Car B										
Car C										
Car D										
Car E										
Knitting										
Phoning										
Reading										
Singing										
Writing										

Car	Driver	Activity

Star Bookings

Not having had a hit for over six months, Carrie Crooner was reluctantly persuaded to get out more and meet the public. Next month she'll be doing just that, as she has been booked to open four new shops in different towns. In which town is each shop located, what does it sell, and on which date will the "Grand Opening by a Singing Star" take place?

1. Carrie has been booked to open the toy shop six days after the date of the grand opening at the shop in Fort George.

2. The shop in Brookford will open later in the month than the one selling clothes, but earlier in the month than The Zone.

3. The shop named Fifteen (after its number on the High Street) will open six days later than the shop in Windridge.

4. Mitchell's is a shoe shop and will be opened either six days before or six days after the shop in Netherton.

	Brookford	Fort George	Netherton	Windridge	Books	Clothes	Shoes	Toys	11th	17th	23rd	29th
Dean & Co												
Fifteen												
Mitchell's												
The Zone												
11th												
17th												
23rd												
29th												
Books												
Clothes												
Shoes												
Toys												

Shop	Town	Sells	Date

Big Babies!

The four women in this puzzle are all expecting babies, but it's their husbands who are suffering with cravings! Each man needs a regular supply of a particular type of food, or he sulks. . . . Discover the name of every woman's husband, when their baby is due, and each man's craving.

1. Debbie, whose husband craves prawns, is expecting a baby two months after David's is due.

2. Jerry's wife is expecting their baby the month before that of the woman (not Martine) whose husband's craving is for cheese.

3. Sam likes to eat salmon for breakfast every morning and supper every night. His baby will be born earlier than (but not the month before) Colin's.

4. Ruth's baby will be born before that of the woman married to Sam.

	Husband				Baby Due				Craving			
	Colin	David	Jerry	Sam	January	February	March	April	Bacon	Cheese	Prawns	Salmon
Caroline												
Debbie												
Martine												
Ruth												
Bacon												
Cheese												
Prawns												
Salmon												
January												
February												
March												
April												

Woman	Husband	Due	Craving

A Moving Story

The five people in this puzzle have all moved to different apartments, although none has moved out of the building (it's just that their new apartments are larger than the old ones). Can you discover the numbers of the apartments each has moved from and to?

1. Mr. White's new number has digits that add up to the same total as that of the digits of his old apartment number.

2. The number of Miss Carter's new apartment is higher than the number of Mr. Mason's old one.

3. The number of Mr. Mason's new apartment is four higher than that of Mrs. Stoker's new one.

4. Mr. Mason's old apartment had a number ten lower than the number of Mr. Havelock's new one.

5. Mrs. Stoker's old number was lower than Mr. Havelock's old one, but higher than that of the person who moved into No. 54.

	Old Apartment					New Apartment				
	43	49	51	59	62	54	58	61	65	69
Miss Carter										
Mr. Havelock										
Mr. Mason										
Mr. Stoker										
Mr. White										
No. 54						
No. 58						
No. 61						
No. 65						
No. 69						

New

Name	Old	New

The Party Season

Johnnie received five invitations this morning, all requesting his attendance at parties to be held next month. Can you link each host to the reason he is holding a party, and the date on which it will take place?

1. Henry's will take place the day after the retirement party.

2. The party being held to celebrate one man's daughter graduating as a doctor will be held later than Philip's function.

3. Jack's party will take place two days before the birthday party.

4. Neil is holding a party four days before that of the man (not Lionel) who is emigrating.

	Reason					Date				
	Birthday	Book launch	Emigration	Graduation	Retirement	7th	9th	10th	11th	13th
Henry										
Jack										
Lionel											
Neil											
Philip											
7th											
9th											
10th											
11th											
13th											

Host	Reason	Date

Odds and Ends

Over the years, the four men in this puzzle have amassed quite a quantity of odd socks, old shirts, and torn trousers. No man has the same number of odd socks as either old shirts or torn pairs of pants, nor has he the same number of old shirts as torn trousers, so in every man's case, there are three different quantities. Can you determine who has what?

1. The man with nine odd socks has one fewer torn pairs of pants than Tony, who has one more old shirt than the man with six odd socks.

2. The man with seven old shirts has one more odd sock than Fred.

3. Marty has fewer old shirts than Vernon.

		Odd Socks				Old Shirts				Torn Pants			
		6	7	9	10	5	7	8	9	8	9	10	11
	Fred												
	Marty												
	Tony												
	Vernon												
Torn Pants	8												
	9												
	10												
	11												
Old Shirts	5												
	7												
	8												
	9												

Man	Socks	Shirts	Pants

Rumor Spreaders

The four women in this puzzle are prone to spreading rumors. Luckily, their rumors are only about one another! For each of the listed rumors, can you discover who did the gossiping, which woman heard the tale, and the name of the woman they were talking about? (Naturally, none of the women started a rumor about herself or about the woman to whom she was speaking!)

1. Alison told a story about the flirtatious nature of one of the women.

2. Chrissie was said to be lazy, but not by Barbara. Nor did Barbara listen to the rumor of Chrissie's laziness.

3. The woman who started the rumor about Diane was the subject of the rumor about gambling, which Chrissie listened to.

		Talker				Listener				About		
	Alison	Barbara	Chrissie	Diane	Alison	Barbara	Chrissie	Diane	Alison	Barbara	Chrissie	Diane
Drinking												
Flirting												
Gambling												
Laziness												
About — Alison												
About — Barbara												
About — Chrissie												
About — Diane												
Listener — Alison												
Listener — Barbara												
Listener — Chrissie												
Listener — Diane												

Rumor	Talker	Listener	About

Split Personalities

In a fit of pique at her poor final exam results Loretta has taken photographs of five of her teachers (listed in the grid below by the subject each teaches), cut each into three pieces (head, body, and legs), and then reassembled them in such a way that each "new" picture contains pieces of three "old" ones. How have the pictures been reassembled?

1. The English teacher's head is now attached to the geography teacher's body.

2. The geography teacher's legs are now attached to the body of the French teacher.

3. The history teacher's head is in the same picture as the science teacher's legs.

4. The French teacher's legs, the history teacher's body, and the geography teacher's head are all in three different "new" pictures.

		Body					Legs				
		English	French	Geography	History	Science	English	French	Geography	History	Science
Head	English										
	French										
	Geography										
	History										
	Science										
Legs	English										
	French										
	Geography										
	History										
	Science										

Head	Body	Legs

Dockside Development

The trendy apartment buildings of Dockside were originally small factories connected with shipbuilding as, until the middle of the 1950s, Dockside was a major shipping and shipbuilding center. The buildings, converted into the most luxurious apartments, line the waterfront and were constructed in the 19th century. What company originally traded at each and what did it produce?

1. Arnott's produced the blocks and tackle needed for the rigging of ships in the building constructed two years later than that where ships' propellers were formerly made.

2. J. J. Forrester occupied the premises built four years earlier than that which constructed ships' lifeboats.

3. The earliest of the five buildings once housed the factory that made pumps.

4. The McDonald's factory (which didn't produce steam engines) was built earlier than the premises of Dagg & Meek.

	Arnott's	Dagg & Meek	J. J. Forrester	McDonald's	Seatrader	Blocks/tackle	Lifeboats	Propellers	Pumps	Steam engines
1882										
1884										
1886										
1890										
1892										
Blocks/tackle										
Lifeboats										
Propellers										
Pumps										
Steam engines										

Built	Company	Produced

Church Funds

The small town of Holyfield has four old churches, all in need of repair. The priest of each church organized a different event last month to raise money for renovations. Every event was well attended by the people of the town, so can you discover the name of the priest at each church, the event he organized, and the amount of money it raised?

1. The priest who organized the church sale raised more money than was collected at St. Mark's Church by the Reverend Lane.

2. The Reverend Carter is not the priest of St. Andrew's, who raised less than the Reverend Thomas (who organized the highly enjoyable three-legged race).

	Priest				Event				Amount			
	Rev. Carter	Rev. Lane	Rev. Thomas	Rev. Walsh	Auction	Church sale	Dance	Three-leg'd race	$1,300	$1,500	$1,700	$1,900
All Saints'												
St. Andrew's												
St. Mark's												
St. Mary's												
$1,300												
$1,500												
$1,700												
$1,900												
Auction												
Church sale												
Dance												
Three-leg'd race												

3. An auction of donated items brought a smile to the face of the priest of All Saints' Church—and $1,700 toward the cost of the repairs to the drains there!

Church	Priest	Event	Amount

Recycling

Following various parties at their homes over the weekend, four people made trips to their local recycling depot, taking with them various quantities of brown, green, and clear glass bottles. Can you determine the numbers taken by each person?

1. Faith took more green bottles (but fewer clear bottles) than the person who took eleven brown bottles.

2. Gordon took two more brown bottles than clear bottles, but fewer green bottles than the person who took eight brown bottles.

3. Jane took one more clear bottle than green bottles, but fewer brown bottles than the person who took six green bottles.

4. Kenneth took one more clear bottle than brown bottles, but fewer green bottles than the person who took seven clear bottles.

	Brown				Green				Clear			
	8	10	11	12	6	7	8	9	7	8	9	11
Faith												
Gordon												
Jane												
Kenneth												
Clear 7												
8												
9												
11												
Green 6												
7												
8												
9												

Name	Brown	Green	Clear

Colorful Line

Five women are in a line waiting for a bus to take them home. Coincidentally, each is wearing a coat, hat, and scarf in three different colors; and none has either a coat, hat, or scarf of the same color as any other woman's. Can you discover the combinations in the colorful line?

1. The woman in the red coat wore a hat of the same color as the scarf worn by the woman in the turquoise coat.

2. The woman with the red scarf wore a hat of the same color as the coat worn by the woman with a turquoise scarf.

3. The woman with the maroon hat wore a coat of the same color as the scarf worn by the woman with a turquoise hat.

4. The woman with the green hat wore a navy blue scarf.

		Hat					Scarf				
		Green	Maroon	Navy	Red	Turquoise	Green	Maroon	Navy	Red	Turquoise
Coat	Green										
	Maroon										
	Navy										
	Red										
	Turquoise										
Scarf	Green										
	Maroon										
	Navy										
	Red										
	Turquoise										

Coat	Hat	Scarf

Check-in

The diagram below shows five check-in desks in the airport departures terminal. Can you match the number of each desk with the destination of the flight it is currently serving, together with the time of the flight?

1. The flight to Oslo isn't due to depart at 12:30 p.m.

2. The flight to Gibraltar takes off thirty minutes later than that being dealt with at Desk 2, but earlier than the flight to Lisbon.

3. The flight to Alicante, Spain, takes off fifteen minutes earlier than that being dealt with at a desk next to that dealing with the flight to Alicante.

4. Desk 4 is dealing with passengers traveling to Singapore and is closer to Passport Control than the desk dealing with passengers bound for Gibraltar.

5. The desk closest to the entrance isn't dealing with passengers for the flight departing at 1:45 p.m.

	Alicante	Gibraltar	Lisbon	Oslo	Singapore	12:30 P.M.	1:00 P.M.	1:15 P.M.	1:45 P.M.	2:00 P.M.
Desk 1										
Desk 2										
Desk 3										
Desk 4										
Desk 5										
12:30 P.M.										
1:00 P.M.										
1:15 P.M.										
1:45 P.M.										
2:00 P.M.										

Entrance

Desk 1
Desk 2
Desk 3
Desk 4
Desk 5

Passport Control

Desk	Destination	Departs

Raffle Prizes

At a recent school fair, Jimmy's four aunts each bought a raffle ticket that won a prize! What was each woman's ticket number, what was its color, and what prize did it win for her?

1. The pink ticket had a number forty-six higher than that which won the clock.

2. The yellow ticket had a lower number than the white ticket, but a higher number than that which won a prize for Jimmy's Aunt Andrea.

3. The green ticket won a very nice pen for one of the aunts.

4. Jimmy's Aunt Sharon won a glass vase. Her ticket number was lower than that bought by Jimmy's Aunt Wendy (who didn't win the cake).

	Ticket				Color				Prize			
	008	054	100	146	Green	Pink	White	Yellow	Cake	Clock	Pen	Vase
Andrea												
Karen												
Sharon												
Wendy												
Cake								
Clock								
Pen								
Vase								
Green				
Pink				
White				
Yellow				

Aunt	Ticket	Color	Prize

Leisurely Gifts

Four men whose birthdays were last week were given leisure-related gifts by their wives. What is the name of each man's wife, what did he receive, and on what day of last week was his birthday?

1. Don's birthday was the day before that of the man who received a magnificent set of new golf clubs (but not from Olivia).

2. Janet gave her husband a fishing rod. His birthday was earlier in the week than Ryan's (which wasn't on Thursday).

3. Harry is a keen astronomer, so he was delighted to receive a powerful new telescope for his birthday, which was later in the week than that of Claire's husband (who isn't Don).

	Wife				Gift				Birthday			
	Claire	Janet	Olivia	Rose	Camera	Fishing rod	Golf clubs	Telescope	Monday	Wednesday	Thursday	Friday
Don												
Harry												
Mark												
Ryan												
Monday												
Wednesday												
Thursday												
Friday												
Camera												
Fishing rod												
Golf clubs												
Telescope												

Husband	Wife	Gift	Birthday

Out and About

Now that Tim has retired from full-time work, he likes to get out and about, visiting various places in town. He goes to each twice per week, once in the afternoon and once in the evening, though he never goes to the same place twice in one day. Where did he go each weekday afternoon and evening last week?

1. Tim didn't go to the library on two consecutive days.

2. Neither of his visits to the social club was on the same day as his trips to either the library or the cinema.

3. It wasn't on Friday that Tim spent the evening at the shops, although his evening visit to the shops was later in the week than his afternoon trip to the swimming pool.

4. Tim's evening outing to the swimming pool was the day after he'd spent the afternoon at the shops, but the day before his evening trip to the cinema (which wasn't on the same day as his afternoon library visit).

	Afternoon					Evening				
	Cinema	Library	Shops	Social club	Swimming pool	Cinema	Library	Shops	Social club	Swimming pool
Monday										
Tuesday										
Wednesday										
Thursday										
Friday										
Cinema					
Library					
Shops					
Social club					
Swimming					

(Evening)

Day	Afternoon	Evening

In Tandem

Jake and Louise have just returned from a country cycling holiday. They cycled a different number of miles per day on a tandem, taking in the views as they traveled from town to town. Can you discover how many miles they cycled each day and the town in which they spent the night, before moving on again the next morning?

1. Jake and Louise cycled two more miles on Thursday than on the day (not Friday) that they traveled to Big River.

2. On Monday they cycled to Waterford, covering more miles than on the day they went to Arkhill (which they didn't visit the day after going to Big River).

3. Directly after leaving Rockfort, Jake and Louise traveled to Edge Point.

4. Jake and Louise covered one more mile on Tuesday than on Wednesday.

	Miles					To (town)				
	19	21	22	24	25	Arkhill	Big River	Edge Point	Rockfort	Waterford
Monday										
Tuesday										
Wednesday										
Thursday										
Friday										
Arkhill										
Big River										
Edge Point										
Rockfort										
Waterford										

Day	Miles	To (town)

Good Reads

Four of Dorothy's relatives have loaned her books to read. Who owns each, what is her relationship to Dorothy, and in what order has Dorothy decided to read the books?

1. The book that Dorothy has borrowed from her aunt will be read earlier than *Water's Edge*.

2. Angela is Dorothy's sister, whose book will be read earlier than *Sanctuary*.

3. Dorothy intends to read her cousin's book first. This isn't *Enigma*, which has been lent to her by Geraldine.

4. The book entitled *Lost Cause* belongs to Candice.

	Woman				Relation				Order			
	Angela	Candice	Fiona	Geraldine	Aunt	Cousin	Mother	Sister	First	Second	Third	Fourth
Enigma												
Lost Cause												
Sanctuary												
Water's Edge												
First												
Second												
Third												
Fourth												
Aunt												
Cousin												
Mother												
Sister												

Title	Woman	Relation	Order

Murder Investigation

Private investigator Tracey Ditch is looking into a case of murder. She has four suspects, all of whom had a possible motive. Can you discover each person's relationship to the deceased (whose name was, appropriately, Ivor Deathwish!), together with the motive and the length of time he or she had known Ivor?

1. Ivor's wife (now his widow) had known him for longer than the man whose possible motive was revenge, having discovered that Ivor had been responsible for a car accident that had killed his son.

2. Harriet was Ivor's lover. Her possible motive wasn't connected with blackmail. Whoever had been the victim of Ivor's blackmail (Ivor could have ruined his or her career) hadn't known him for twenty-one years.

	Relation				Motive				Time (years)			
	Business pthr.	Cousin	Lover	Wife	Blackmail	Jealousy	Money	Revenge	6	11	16	21
Gary												
Harriet												
Sheila												
Vincent												
6 years												
11 years												
16 years												
21 years												
Blackmail												
Jealousy												
Money												
Revenge												

3. Vincent had known Ivor for five fewer years than his business partner, who owed Ivor a lot of money, thus stood to gain financially from his death.

Suspect	Relation	Motive	Time

Stamp Collection

This morning there were just five customers who bought postage stamps at the Highfield General Store and each bought a different quantity, thus providing us with facts for this puzzle! In what order did each customer arrive and how many stamps did he or she purchase?

1. Ian arrived later than the person who bought ten stamps, who arrived directly before Hans.

2. The person who arrived second bought one fewer stamp than Rosie, who arrived later than the person who bought the most stamps.

3. Lola arrived later than the person who bought three more stamps than Sean.

	Order					Stamps				
	First	Second	Third	Fourth	Fifth	9	10	12	13	15
Hans										
Ian										
Lola										
Rosie										
Sean										
9 stamps					
10 stamps					
12 stamps					
13 stamps					
15 stamps					

Customer	Order	Stamps

Shoe Sales

Imelda can't resist buying new footwear, so when the sales were on last week, she threw caution to the wind and bought another five pairs of shoes (all of the footwear bought in this puzzle is referred to as "shoes"). Can you work out which shoes were bought each day and from which shop?

1. The slippers were bought the day before the shoes from Heale's, but later in the week than her visit to Sharp's Shoes.

2. Tuesday's purchase was of a pair of riding boots.

3. Imelda made a purchase from Cosy-Fit the day after she bought a pair of leather sandals.

4. The stilettos were bought earlier in the week than the trainers. Neither of these two pairs of shoes came from Heale's.

5. The purchase from Shoe Box was made the day after she bought a pair of shoes from In-Step.

	Boots	Sandals	Slippers	Stilettos	Trainers	Cosy-Fit	In-Step	Heale's	Sharp's Shoes	Shoe Box
Monday										
Tuesday										
Wednesday										
Thursday										
Friday										
Cosy-Fit										
In-Step										
Heale's										
Sharp's Shoes										
Shoe Box										

Day	Type	Shop

Cinema Treat

As a birthday treat, four children were each taken to the cinema on a different day by one of their relatives. Can you discover when and with whom each child went to the cinema and the type of film he or she chose?

1. Ruth went to the cinema two days later than the child (not Mary) who chose the historical drama film.

2. The child who was treated by an aunt went to the cinema the day before Patrick.

3. The child who was treated by an older brother went to the cinema later in the week than Mary, but earlier in the week than the child who chose the western.

4. One child was taken (by an uncle) to see a comedy film earlier in the week than Johnnie's trip to the cinema.

	Day				Relation				Genre			
	Monday	Tuesday	Wednesday	Thursday	Aunt	Brother	Sister	Uncle	Comedy	Historical	Sci-fi	Western
Johnnie												
Mary												
Patrick												
Ruth												
Comedy												
Historical												
Sci-fi												
Western												
Aunt												
Brother												
Sister												
Uncle												

Child	Day	Relation	Genre

Poster Pickups

Four people went into Paula's Poster Shop in town yesterday and bought a poster for a child's bedroom. Who purchased each of the differently priced posters, to whom will it be given, and what is depicted on each?

1. Cheryl paid thirty cents more for her poster than the price paid for the poster that will hang on Marilyn's bedroom wall.

2. The poster of the hockey player wasn't the most expensive, although it did cost more than the one that will adorn the wall of Neil's bedroom.

3. The picture of a tiger was bought for Carl, but not by Philip.

4. Norma bought a poster for Zoë's bedroom.

5. The poster bought by Dave features two adorable cocker spaniel puppies.

	Buyer				For			Subject			
	Cheryl	Dave	Norma	Philip	Carl	Marilyn	Neil	Zoë	Hockey player	Pop singer	Puppies	Tiger
$4.20												
$4.50												
$4.80												
$5.00												
Hockey player												
Pop singer												
Puppies												
Tiger												
Carl												
Marilyn												
Neil												
Zoë												

Price	Buyer	For	Subject

The Boys Next Door

The map below shows five houses, each of which is home to one of five schoolboys, who are great friends. What is the full name of the boy who lives at each address?

1. Ben's house has a number two lower than that of the boy surnamed Wheeler, who lives in the house directly opposite that occupied by Max and his family.

2. The boy surnamed Myers lives in a house directly next door to that occupied by Derek and his family, who live directly opposite the home of the Dane family.

3. Timothy's house has a number one lower than Ray's. Ray's surname isn't Smith.

	Boy					Surname				
	Ben	Derek	Max	Ray	Timothy	Clark	Dane	Myers	Smith	Wheeler
No. 6										
No. 7										
No. 8										
No. 9										
No. 10										
Clark					
Dane					
Myers					
Smith					
Wheeler					

No. 7 No. 9

Lad's Lane

No. 6 No. 8 No. 10

House No.	Boy	Surname

Split Personalities

Doctor Strangezoo has been experimenting with animals. He has taken photographs of five and cut each into three pieces (head, body, and legs) and then reassembled them in such a way that each "new" picture contains pieces of three "old" ones. How have the pictures been reassembled?

1. The cat's body now balances precariously on the ducks' legs.

2. The dog's head is now attached to the body of the horse.

3. The dog's legs are in the same picture as the tiger's head.

4. The legs of the animal whose body now has the horse's head are now with the head of the duck.

5. The dog's body is not in the same picture as the cat's legs.

		Body					Legs				
		Cat	Dog	Duck	Horse	Tiger	Cat	Dog	Duck	Horse	Tiger
Head	Cat										
	Dog										
	Duck										
	Horse										
	Tiger										
Legs	Cat										
	Dog										
	Duck										
	Horse										
	Tiger										

Head	Body	Legs

Racing Dogs

Four people decided to race their dogs against one another. The dogs were reluctant to start, but eventually were persuaded to run. Each dog is of a different age and wore a collar of a different color. Can you piece together all of the facts, and also learn each dog's finishing position in the race?

1. Zach finished immediately ahead of the dog in the yellow collar, which didn't finish fourth and isn't the youngest dog.

2. The youngest dog finished immediately ahead of the dog in the green collar, which is two months older than Floss. Floss didn't wear the red collar.

3. The dog (not Bobby) in the blue collar is older than the one that won the race.

	15 months	17 months	18 months	19 months	Blue	Green	Red	Yellow	First	Second	Third	Fourth
Bobby												
Floss												
Misty												
Zach												
First												
Second												
Third												
Fourth												
Blue												
Green												
Red												
Yellow												

Dog	Age	Collar	Finished

Colorful Cocktails

It's Barbara's pre-wedding party night and she and four friends are celebrating at the local nightclub. Wanting to keep a clear head for tomorrow morning, Barbara is only drinking fruit juice, but her friends have ordered the drinks lined up as you see in the diagram below. The cocktails are all of different colors, and have strange names, but the clues will help you identify them, and discover who ordered each.

1. The Sky High is further left than the drink ordered by Helen, but further right than the bubbly orange concoction.

2. The strange-looking blue drink ordered by Sarah is further right than the Kick Start.

3. Laura has ordered a Lazy Slurp, which is pictured between two other cocktails, neither of which was ordered by Brenda.

4. Cocktail C isn't purple in color.

	Blue	Green	Orange	Purple	Duck's Fizz	Kick Start	Lazy Slurp	Sky High	Brenda	Helen	Laura	Sarah
Cocktail A												
Cocktail B												
Cocktail C												
Cocktail D												
Brenda												
Helen												
Laura												
Sarah												
Duck's Fizz												
Kick Start												
Lazy Slurp												
Sky High												

LEFT ⇐   RIGHT ⇒

A B C D

Cocktail	Color	Name	Drinker

Children's Ailments

The children in this puzzle are all absent from school at the moment, suffering from various ailments. Can you decide each child's full name, and the illness he or she has?

1. Tina is suffering from the mumps at the moment. Neither she nor Karen is the child surnamed Jarvis.

2. The child surnamed Wilder has contracted tonsillitis.

3. The little boy whose surname is Peters has chicken pox.

4. Oliver Blane isn't the child suffering from a mild attack of influenza.

	Surname					Illness				
	Arden	Blane	Jarvis	Peters	Wilder	Chicken pox	Influenza	Measles	Mumps	Tonsillitis
Adam										
Joanna										
Karen										
Oliver										
Tina										
Chicken pox					
Influenza					
Measles					
Mumps					
Tonsillitis					

Child	Surname	Ailment

Roving Reporter

Daily Globe reporter Ivor Presspass spent Monday to Friday of last week in South America, interviewing film stars who were visiting different countries. Can you decide the country in which he interviewed each celebrity, together with the day on which he did so?

1. Ivor's meeting with Carlos Kato took place earlier in the week than his trip to Argentina, but two days after he had interviewed Paul Porter.

2. The interview with Bella Jones took place more than one day before he met with Jim O'Neill.

3. Ivor flew to Chile later in the week than he went to Ecuador, but the day before he met up with Samuel Smith in Peru.

4. Neither Bella Jones nor Paul Porter was interviewed in Brazil.

	Argentina	Brazil	Chile	Ecuador	Peru	Monday	Tuesday	Wednesday	Thursday	Friday
Bella Jones										
Carlos Kato										
Jim O'Neill										
Paul Porter										
Samuel Smith										
Monday										
Tuesday										
Wednesday										
Thursday										
Friday										

Star	Country	Day

Anniversary Cruises

Four couples are each celebrating their wedding anniversary by taking a cruise to an exotic location, aboard a luxury liner. Can you match each husband and wife to the anniversary they are celebrating and the name of the ship on which they are cruising?

1. Denise and her husband have been married for longer than twenty-five years, so they aren't celebrating their silver wedding anniversary.

2. Grace isn't married to Arthur; and Richard isn't married to Camilla.

3. Felicity and her husband are enjoying their cruise aboard the *Ocean Winner*.

4. Richard is aboard the *Sea Sprite*, but not with Grace.

5. The couple celebrating their ruby wedding anniversary are on the *Ocean Breeze*, cruising the Mediterranean, unlike Paul and his wife.

6. Arthur and his wife (who isn't Felicity) are celebrating their diamond wedding anniversary.

	Wife				Anniversary				Ship			
	Camilla	Denise	Felicity	Grace	Diamond	Golden	Ruby	Silver	Ocean Breeze	Ocean Winner	Sea Queen	Sea Sprite
Arthur												
Paul												
Richard												
Terry												
Ocean Breeze												
Ocean Winner												
Sea Queen												
Sea Sprite												
Diamond												
Golden												
Ruby												
Silver												

Husband	Wife	Anniv.	Ship

Chair Arrangement

In the Sofa So Good sale there are four sofas lined up in the window, each on sale at a special price. All are covered in a different material and each is of a different color and price to the rest. Can you match the details to the sofas in the diagram of the shop window, as shown below?

1. The blue sofa is next to and between the one covered in a cotton fabric (which isn't burgundy in color) and the most expensive sofa.

2. The leather sofa is further left than that on sale at $199.

3. The cream sofa is next to and between the one priced at $179 and that with chenille covers.

4. Sofa D (which isn't green) is on sale at a price twenty dollars less than sofa C.

	Material				Color				Price			
	Chintz	Chenille	Cotton	Leather	Blue	Burgundy	Cream	Green	$159	$179	$199	$229
Sofa A												
Sofa B												
Sofa C												
Sofa D												
$159												
$179												
$199												
$229												
Blue												
Burgundy												
Cream												
Green												

LEFT ⇦   RIGHT ⇨

A   B   C   D

Sofa	Material	Color	Price

Telephone Expenses

The five people in this puzzle spent rather a lot of time on the telephone over the Christmas period last year, making calls to friends and members of their families. Can you discover how many calls each made on Christmas Eve and Christmas Day?

1. Whoever made nine calls on Christmas Eve made two fewer calls than Freda on Christmas Day.

2. Whoever made six calls on Christmas Day made two fewer calls than Hal on Christmas Eve.

3. Iris made two more calls on Christmas Day than Jimmy made on Christmas Eve.

4. Graeme made a total of more than seventeen calls. He didn't make the same number of calls on Christmas Day as Freda made on Christmas Eve.

	Christmas Eve Calls					Christmas Day Calls				
	6	7	8	9	10	5	6	7	8	9
Freda										
Graeme										
Hal										
Iris										
Jimmy										
5 calls										
6 calls										
7 calls										
8 calls										
9 calls										

Day

Caller	Eve	Day

Serving Time

The cell block shown in the diagram below is home to five thieves, each serving a different sentence for his part in the Benchester Bank robbery, which made headline news last year. Who is the occupant of each numbered cell and what is his sentence?

1. Dan Digby is in the cell directly opposite that of the man serving twenty-two years for his part in the robbery.

2. The man (not John Fox) who was awarded the shortest sentence is in a cell directly next to that of the man serving the longest sentence.

3. The man in cell 5 was given a sentence two years longer than another of the robbers, but shorter than that given to Phil Grant.

4. Roger Plum's sentence is three years longer than that given to the occupant of cell 3.

5. Sam White's cell number is three higher than that of John Fox.

	Criminal					Sentence (years)				
	Dan Digby	John Fox	Phil Grant	Roger Plum	Sam White	15	18	20	22	25
Cell 1										
Cell 2										
Cell 3										
Cell 4										
Cell 5										
15 years										
18 years										
20 years										
22 years										
25 years										

4	3
5	2
	1

Cell	Criminal	Sentence

Medallion Man

Most women have met Medallion Man at some time or another: silk shirt open to the waist, smooth image, all the chat, and a gold medallion at his neck! Pat Frazes is such a man. No matter how many brush-offs he gets from the women he approaches, he's always ready to try again. Who did he try to pick up on each of four evenings last week, where was she at the time, and what was her reply?

1. Cathy was unfortunate enough to meet Pat at a party and Naomi encountered him at a college dance.

2. Pat was told to "Get lost!" the evening before his encounter with the woman who told him to "Take a dive!" at the swimming pool.

3. Thursday evening's encounter with Bella wasn't at the nightclub.

4. Elaine's response to Pat's overtures was to tell him to "Clear off!". His meeting with Elaine was the evening before the party.

	Woman				Place				Reply			
	Bella	Cathy	Elaine	Naomi	Dance	Nightclub	Party	Swimming pool	"Clear off!"	"Get lost!"	"Shove off!"	"Take a dive!"
Wednesday												
Thursday												
Friday												
Saturday												
"Clear off!"												
"Get lost!"												
"Shove off!"												
"Take a dive!"												
Dance												
Nightclub												
Party												
Swimming pool												

Evening	Woman	Place	Reply

The Snowman

Four children made the snowman you see below, each providing a different item with which to "dress" him. What is the surname and age of each child, and which item(s) did he or she contribute?

1. The child surnamed Ford is older than the one who gave up his or her woolly hat in order to keep the snowman warm.

2. Darren is nine years of age. His surname starts with a later letter of the alphabet than Andrew's, but an earlier letter of the alphabet than that of the child who provided the broom.

3. Anna is younger than the child surnamed Player, but older than the child who provided a carrot for the snowman's nose and stones for his eyes.

	Surname				Age				Item(s)			
	Cliff	Ford	Marks	Player	7	8	9	10	Broom	Hat	Nose/eyes	Scarf
Andrew												
Anna												
Darren												
Donna												
Broom												
Hat												
Nose/eyes												
Scarf												
7												
8												
9												
10												

Age

Child	Surname	Age	Item(s)

Benny the Bee

Benny the bumblebee was busy this morning, visiting several clumps of flowers in the garden. In the space of twenty minutes, he visited five different flowers in various locations, leaving for a different reason every time. Which flower was visited at each of the listed times and what caused Benny to move on?

1. Noisy children caused Benny to move from one group of flowers directly to the jasmine nearby. Birds weren't the cause of Benny's move from the jasmine.

2. The roses were investigated immediately before the flowers that Benny had to abandon due to a very short-lived burst of rain.

3. Ten minutes after Benny stopped at the lavender, he was chased away from another group of plants by birds, which had settled on the tree overhead.

4. Benny stopped to savor the mimosa (which wasn't the last clump of flowers he visited) later than he had settled on the carnations.

5. The first move wasn't due to the encounter with the cat.

	Carnations	Jasmine	Lavender	Mimosa	Roses	Birds	Cat	Children	No more nectar	Rain
10:00 A.M.										
10:05 A.M.										
10:10 A.M.										
10:15 A.M.										
10:20 A.M.										
Birds										
Cat										
Children										
No more nectar										
Rain										

Time	Flowers	Reason

Swan Lake

Five injured swans were brought in to the Swan Lake Sanctuary last week. Each had a different injury and arrived on a different day—and we are happy to report that each is making progress toward full recovery. Can you match the name given to each swan with its injury and day of arrival?

1. The swan covered in oil arrived at the sanctuary before the one that had swallowed a fish hook.

2. The swan with an injured beak arrived on Wednesday, which was earlier in the week than the day that Samson was brought in.

3. Delilah isn't the swan with the damaged wing, brought in on Monday.

4. The swan with a broken leg was brought in the day before Sheba, who was brought in the day before Jezebel.

	Broken leg	Damaged wing	Fish hook	Injured beak	Oil on feathers	Monday	Tuesday	Wednesday	Thursday	Friday
Delilah										
Jezebel										
Samson										
Sheba										
Solomon										
Monday					
Tuesday					
Wednesday					
Thursday					
Friday					

Swan	Injury	Arrived

Bedtime

Four sisters are getting ready for bed and are just about to brush their teeth and get into their pajamas. No girl has a toothbrush of the same color as her pajamas, so can you relate each sister to the color of her toothbrush, as well as the color of her pajamas and which pattern is printed onto them?

1. Anne's toothbrush is of the same color as the pajamas with a pattern of spots.

2. Betty's pajamas are pale green and haven't a pattern of spots.

3. The girl with an orange toothbrush has striped pajamas of the same color as Dawn's toothbrush. Dawn's pajamas aren't blue and haven't a pattern of stars.

4. The girl with a blue toothbrush has a pair of white pajamas. She isn't Cara; nor is Cara's toothbrush green.

	Toothbrush				Pajamas				Pattern			
	Blue	Green	Orange	White	Blue	Green	Orange	White	Flowers	Spots	Stars	Stripes
Anne												
Betty												
Cara												
Dawn												
Flowers												
Spots												
Stars												
Stripes												
Blue													
Green													
Orange													
White													

Sister	T'brush	Pajamas	Pattern

Playing Cards

The four men in this puzzle are playing a game of cards and each has three in his hand: one diamond, one heart and one spade. Can you discover which three cards are in each man's hand? (Note—A = ace, J = jack, Q = queen, and K = king; and in the game ace = 1, jack = 11, queen = 12, king = 13, and the values of the other cards are as per their numbers.)

1. The man with the king of spades has a heart with a value three higher than that of the heart held by Ian, but a lower value than that of the diamond held by Harry.

2. John's diamond has a lower value than that of his heart (which isn't the seven).

3. The man with the four of hearts has a spade with a value three lower than that of John's spade.

4. Ian's diamond has a lower value than that of Harry's spade.

5. The man with the ace of hearts doesn't have the queen of diamonds.

	Diamond				Heart				Spade			
	2	3	J	Q	A	4	7	J	3	7	10	K
Harry												
Ian												
John												
Kenny												
Spade 3												
Spade 7												
Spade 10												
Spade K												
Heart A									
Heart 4									
Heart 7									
Heart J									

Player	Diamond	Heart	Spade

Getting Fit

After using her weighing machine and being surprised by the reading, Emma decided to enroll in some fitness classes. She has joined five and her first sessions are all at different times on different days next week. Can you discover the time and day each class takes place?

1. The trampoline session starts three hours later than the class held two days after the class with the earliest starting time.

2. Wednesday's session starts thirty minutes later than the yoga class, which is held the day before the class starting at eleven o'clock.

3. Friday's step exercise class begins at a later time than either Thursday's session or the aerobics class (which isn't on Thursday).

	Time					Day				
	10:30 A.M.	11:00 A.M.	11:30 A.M.	2:00 P.M.	2:30 P.M.	Tuesday	Wednesday	Thursday	Friday	Saturday
Aerobics										
Step										
Swimming										
Trampoline										
Yoga										
Tuesday										
Wednesday										
Thursday										
Friday										
Saturday										

Class	Time	Day

Job Swap

As part of a community awareness scheme, the five men in this puzzle have all swapped jobs for the day, each doing work usually done by one of the others. Can you discover what everyone does for a living and what he is doing today?

1. The man delivering mail today normally works as a porter in one of the town's largest hotels.

2. Thomas has a very good knowledge (and an equally good map!) of the town, so agreed to take the place of the taxi driver for one day.

3. Gordon has been an office cleaner for the past seven years.

4. David is a waiter at a local restaurant today. The man whose usual job is that of waiter is today doing the job that Kevin would usually do.

	Usual Job					Today				
	Cleaner	Driver	Porter	Postman	Waiter	Cleaner	Driver	Porter	Postman	Waiter
David										
Gordon										
Kevin										
Lou										
Thomas										
Cleaner										
Driver										
Porter										
Postman										
Waiter										

(Today)

Name	Usual Job	Today

Taxi!

Ever since Larry van Truk got his new minivan, his four children have treated him as a taxi driver, pleading for lifts here, there, and everywhere. Over the past few evenings, a different child needed to be brought home from a friend's house, all a different number of miles away; and each also wanted to stop off to buy an item from the shops on the way home. Travel through the clues to discover the details.

1. Friday's trip was one mile further than Larry drove on the night he had to stop to allow one of his children to buy chocolate, peppermints, and a selection of other candy.

2. George asked his dad to stop off at the bookshop, so that he could collect and pay for a book he had ordered. This was the evening before Larry drove four miles, but not the evening after Brendan was collected.

3. Brendan's friend lives five miles from the van Truk household. Colleen's friend lives further away than that of the child (not Brendan) who bought a comic on Saturday evening.

	Child				Kms				Item			
	Brendan	Colleen	George	Marianne	4	5	6	8	Book	Candy	Comic	Lemonade
Wednesday												
Thursday												
Friday												
Saturday												
Book												
Candy												
Comic												
Lemonade												
4 miles												
5 miles												
6 miles												
8 miles												

Evening	Child	Miles	Item

Fitness Fanatics

The four men in this puzzle like to stay fit and active. Last week each cycled, swam, and walked on three different days; and none did the same thing on the same day as anyone else. Can you discover the days on which every man exercised?

1. The man who swam on Monday cycled the day after Stephan cycled.

2. Arthur cycled the day after Bill swam.

3. Bill swam the day after Stephan went for a long walk.

4. Frank swam on the day that Bill cycled, which was the day after Arthur had taken his walk.

		Cycled				Swam				Walked			
		Wednesday	Thursday	Friday	Saturday	Monday	Tuesday	Thursday	Friday	Tuesday	Wednesday	Thursday	Friday
	Arthur												
	Bill												
	Frank												
	Stephan												
Walked	Tuesday												
	Wednesday												
	Thursday												
	Friday												
Swam	Monday												
	Tuesday												
	Thursday												
	Friday												

Man	Cycled	Swam	Walked

Sales

Five local shops have announced sales beginning on different days next week. Follow the clues to discover at what time, and on which day each starts.

1. The sale that begins on Wednesday starts at a time either fifteen minutes earlier or fifteen minutes later than the starting time of Thursday's sale.

2. The shop with a sale starting at ten o'clock doesn't open on Mondays.

3. The sale at the music shop isn't scheduled to start at half past eight.

4. The book shop sale begins on Friday, at either 9:00 a.m. or 9:30 a.m.

5. The shop with a sale beginning on Tuesday starts its sale within thirty minutes of the starting time of the toy shop sale.

6. The sale starting at 9:15 a.m. begins the day after the shoe shop sale.

	Monday	Tuesday	Wednesday	Thursday	Friday	8:30 A.M.	9:00 A.M.	9:15 A.M.	9:30 A.M.	10:00 A.M.
Book shop										
Clothing shop										
Music shop										
Shoe shop										
Toy shop										
8:30 A.M.										
9:00 A.M.										
9:15 A.M.										
9:30 A.M.										
10:00 A.M.										

Shop	Day	Time

Dolls' Hospital

In response to a local radio appeal five young women have decided to donate their dolls to the children's ward of a nearby hospital because the women feel they no longer have a need for dolls! However, each woman has decided not to part with her favorite. Can you discover how many dolls each woman will be giving, together with the name of the one doll she will keep?

1. Harriet (who is donating two fewer dolls than Christine) isn't keeping the doll named Serena.

2. Danielle is donating one more doll than the woman who decided that she really couldn't bear to part with Bella.

3. Nicola is giving fewer dolls than the woman keeping Angelique, but more dolls than the woman (not Josie) whose favorite is Serena.

4. Tilly belongs to the woman giving ten dolls to the hospital.

| | No. of Dolls | | | | | Keeping | | | | |
	7	8	10	11	12	Angelique	Bella	Jessica	Serena	Tilly
Christine										
Danielle										
Harriet										
Josie										
Nicola										
Angelique										
Bella						
Jessica						
Serena						
Tilly						

Woman	No. of Dolls	Keeping

Rodeo

The Rocking B Ranch Rodeo takes place every year in April. Only the four men lined up in the diagram below were foolhardy enough to attempt to ride Lightning (the unbroken stallion) and all came off in less than a minute. Can you identify each rider, work out his age, and discover the number of seconds he managed to stay in the saddle?

1. Danny managed to stay in the saddle for longer than the oldest man.

2. The twenty-two-year-old stayed on Lightning for longer than someone who is further right than him in the picture below.

3. Chuck stayed on Lightning for less time than the twenty-five-year-old (who is pictured between two of the riders).

4. Joe stayed on for either seven or fourteen fewer seconds than rider A. Rider B is older than the man who stayed on for the shortest time.

5. The man who stayed on longest is pictured next to Scott.

6. The youngest man's name starts with a letter later in the alphabet than that of a man who is further right than him.

	Name				Age				Seconds			
	Chuck	Danny	Joe	Scott	20	22	25	28	35	41	48	55
Rider A												
Rider B												
Rider C												
Rider D												
35 seconds												
41 seconds												
48 seconds												
55 seconds												
20												
22												
25												
28												

Age

LEFT ⟸   RIGHT ⟹

A   B   C   D

Rider	Name	Age	Seconds

What's in a Name?

In each of the families in this puzzle, the initial letters of the names of the husband, wife, and daughter and that of their shared surname start with four different letters of the alphabet. Can you determine the make up for each family?

1. Miss Mitchell's mother has a name that starts with the same letter as that of Robert's surname.

2. Susan's surname starts with a different letter than that of the name of Mandy's daughter.

3. Rachel isn't Patricia's daughter.

	Husband				Wife				Daughter			
	Mike	Peter	Robert	Saul	Mandy	Patricia	Rosemary	Sally	Moira	Priscilla	Rachel	Susan
Mitchell												
Pringle												
Rothman												
Sanders												
Moira												
Priscilla												
Rachel												
Susan												
Mandy												
Patricia												
Rosemary												
Sally												

(left labels: Daughter for Moira–Susan; Wife for Mandy–Sally)

Surname	Husband	Wife	Daughter

Split Personalities

Naughty Norma has cut photographs of five of her relatives each into three pieces (head, body, and legs) and then reassembled them in such a way that each "new" picture contains pieces of three "old" ones. How have the pictures been reassembled?

1. Norma's grandpa's head is in the same picture as her sister's body.

2. Her grandpa's body is in the same picture as her uncle's legs.

3. Her grandpa's legs are in the same picture as her aunt's head.

4. Norma's cousin's head is in the same picture as the body of a male relative, but not her grandpa.

5. Norma's uncle's head is in a different picture to her cousin's legs.

		Body					Legs				
		Aunt	Cousin	Grandpa	Sister	Uncle	Aunt	Cousin	Grandpa	Sister	Uncle
Head	Aunt										
	Cousin										
	Grandpa										
	Sister										
	Uncle										
Legs	Aunt										
	Cousin										
	Grandpa										
	Sister										
	Uncle										

Head	Body	Legs

Piles of Ironing

These five people all do their laundry on a Monday and their ironing later in the week. Can you discover on which different day each does his or her ironing and the total number of items he or she ironed last week?

1. Simon ironed either one more or one fewer item than Wendy.

2. Wendy did her ironing earlier in the week than the person who ironed one fewer item than Wendy.

3. Alison ironed either three more or three fewer items than the person who did the ironing two days later than Margaret (who ironed more than ten items).

4. Brian ironed one more item than the person who did the ironing the day after Alison.

5. The person who did the ironing on Tuesday ironed fewer items than Alison.

| | Day | | | | | No. of Items | | | | |
	Tuesday	Wednesday	Thursday	Friday	Saturday	10	11	13	14	15
Alison										
Brian										
Margaret										
Simon										
Wendy										
10 items					
11 items					
13 items					
14 items					
15 items					

Name	Day	Items

Rare Finds

Four extremely rare coins were discovered during the excavation of various temple sites. They are now on display in the Byzantine Museum, in the arrangement you see in the diagram below. Each coin has a different face value and was found in a different year. Can you match the position of each coin with these details, and say where it was unearthed?

1. The coin found close to the Temple of Zeus is further right than that located in 1933.

2. The 50 Fortunas coin is further left than (but not next to) that discovered near the Temple of Artemis.

3. The 20 Fortunas coin is somewhere between that unearthed in 1951 and the one which came to light in 1972.

4. The earliest find is further right than (but not next to) the 10 Fortunas coin. The coin found at the Temple of Hera isn't next to that discovered in 1951.

5. The coin with the lowest value is further right than that located near the Temple of Athena. The latter is somewhere between the coin found in 1933 and the 20 Fortunas coin.

	Value (Fortunas)				Found				Temple			
	5	10	20	50	1919	1933	1951	1972	Artemis	Athena	Hera	Zeus
Coin A												
Coin B												
Coin C												
Coin D												
Artemis												
Athena												
Hera												
Zeus												
1919												
1933												
1951												
1972												

LEFT ⇦   RIGHT ⇨

(A) (B) (C) (D)

Coin	Value	Found	Temple

Getting Around

The four sales representatives at Puzzleton Products were out on three days last week, doing business in various towns across the country. Each undertook just one trip per day and none visited any town more than once, nor went to a town being visited by one of the other representatives that day. Where did each go every day?

1. The woman who went to Kingston on Wednesday went to Ajax on the day that Roger traveled to Kingston.

2. Kate went to Whitby two days after another representative traveled there.

3. Penny's visit to Newcastle was later in the week than her trip to Ajax.

4. One of the representatives traveled to Whitby on Monday, Newcastle on Wednesday, and Ajax on Friday.

5. Roger didn't go to Newcastle on Monday.

	Monday				Wednesday				Friday			
	Ajax	Kingston	Whitby	Newcastle	Ajax	Kingston	Newcastle	Whitby	Ajax	Kingston	Newcastle	Whitby
Adam												
Kate												
Penny												
Roger												
Friday — Ajax												
Kingston												
Newcastle												
Whitby												
Wednesday — Ajax												
Kingston												
Newcastle												
Whitby												

Rep.	Monday	Wednesday	Friday

Unlucky Numbers

Each week there is a raffle at the Senior Citizens' club in Golden Square and five prizes are awarded to the holders of the winning tickets. Tickets have numbers, which were chosen by the participants, and which do not normally change. However, never having won a thing, five members of the club asked for new numbers. They still haven't won anything, but you don't need luck to discover their old and new numbers: all you need are some clues . . .

1. Steve exchanged his number for a lower one; and Pamela exchanged hers for a number seven higher.

2. David's old number was seven higher than Nicholas's new number.

3. Edith's new number is higher than Nicholas's new number; but Edith's new number is lower than her old number.

4. The difference between Steve's old and new numbers isn't sixteen.

	Old Number					New Number				
	22	31	54	73	81	29	38	66	74	99
David										
Edith										
Nicholas										
Pamela										
Steve										
29										
38										
66										
74										
99										

New

Member	Old Number	New Number

Swimming Session

Five boys visited a local swimming pool yesterday afternoon, each spending a different length of time in the pool, splashing about, and generally having fun. The children also did some more serious swimming and each covered a different number of lengths of the pool. Can you find out how long each spent in the water, and the total number of lengths he swam?

1. Alan was in the pool for five minutes longer than Charlie, who swam two more lengths of the pool than Liam, who didn't spend the longest time in the water.

2. The boy who swam three lengths was in the pool for ten minutes longer than the boy who swam four lengths.

3. Charlie was in the water for ten minutes longer than Graham.

4. Graham swam one fewer length than Ian, who wasn't in the pool for fifty minutes.

	Minutes					Lengths				
	30	35	40	45	50	2	3	4	5	6
Alan										
Charlie										
Graham										
Ian										
Liam										
2 lengths										
3 lengths										
4 lengths										
5 lengths										
6 lengths										

Swimmer	Minutes	Lengths

Honors Night

At the annual Honors Night at school, four of Mr. Walker's nephews were lined up to receive certificates of merit for subjects in which they had excelled during the academic year. A copy of Mr. Walker's photograph of the boys is shown below. Can you discover the identity of each boy, the subject in which he excels, and the percentage of correct answers he gave in a recent examination on that subject?

1. Of the four boys in the photograph: one is boy A; one is Jake; one excels at art; and the other achieved an examination result 2 percent higher than Victor's (which wasn't in art or history).

2. Of the four boys in the photograph: one is boy B; one is Chris; one excels in history; and one achieved a mark 4 percent lower than Chris's result.

3. Of the four boys in the photograph: one is boy C; one is Victor; one excels in geography; and one achieved 90 percent in his examination.

	Chris	Jake	Neil	Victor	Art	Geography	History	Science	88	90	92	94
Boy A												
Boy B												
Boy C												
Boy D												
88%												
90%												
92%												
94%												
Art												
Geography												
History												
Science												

LEFT ⇦   RIGHT ⇨

A B C D

Boy	Name	Subject	Exam %

Basket Cases

After visiting the shop near the main entrance to Puzzleford General Hospital, four visitors arrived in Blackberry Ward bearing small baskets of fruit. No two baskets contained exactly the same quantity of a particular type of fruit (for example, no two baskets both contained three bananas) and in every basket there were three different quantities of the three types of fruit. Can you discover what was in each basket?

1. The basket with four apples contained one more orange than the basket with five bananas, which contained one fewer apple than the basket with six bananas (which wasn't basket B).

2. Basket A contained one more apple than the number of oranges in basket B.

3. Basket C contained one more orange than the number of bananas in basket D.

4. The basket with four bananas didn't also contain five apples.

	Apples				Bananas				Oranges			
	2	3	4	5	3	4	5	6	2	3	4	5
Basket A												
Basket B												
Basket C												
Basket D												
2 oranges												
3 oranges												
4 oranges												
5 oranges												
3 bananas												
4 bananas												
5 bananas												
6 bananas												

Basket	Apples	Bananas	Oranges

Fundraising

Five friends who work together at the local hospital have organized a dance to help raise funds for the new children's ward. Can you match each with her occupation and the number of tickets she has sold to date?

1. The woman who works as a cook has sold seven more tickets than Leanne, but fewer than the midwife.

2. Bridget has sold three fewer tickets than Denise.

3. Amanda has sold more tickets than Leanne, who isn't a nurse.

4. Sally has sold either ten or twenty fewer tickets than the physician.

	Cleaner	Cook	Midwife	Nurse	Physician	35	38	45	52	55
Amanda										
Bridget										
Denise										
Leanne										
Sally										
35 tickets					
38 tickets					
45 tickets					
52 tickets					
55 tickets					

Friend	Occupation	Tickets

Peter's Pots

Peter Porter is a potter. Last week he made five pots at the rate of one per day. He has now displayed them for sale in the window of his shop, as you can see on the diagram below. Can you discover the pattern painted on each pot, together with its price?

1. The pot with a floral design is fifty cents more expensive than pot A.

2. The pot priced at $61 is on a higher shelf (and is further right) than the pot painted with a zigzag pattern.

3. Pot B has been painted with diamonds of various colors and has a price one dollar more than that with a design of bright yellow squares.

4. Pot C has a price two dollars higher than that painted with a pattern of gold and silver stars.

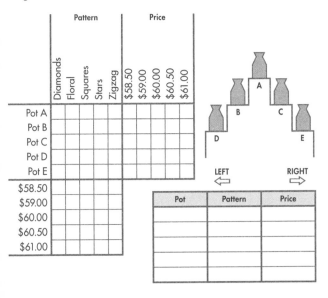

Rooms to Rent

Roberta has just moved to Puzzleford and is looking for rooms to rent. She viewed four premises on Saturday and was quite impressed with them, so is now studying the details in order to make up her mind. At what time was her appointment at each of the listed addresses, what is the rent, and how long would it take Roberta to travel between each and her new place of work?

1. It would take Roberta five minutes longer to get to work from the rooms she saw at three o'clock than from those where the rent is fifty dollars higher than at the rooms seen at three o'clock (which aren't in Keats Court).

2. Roberta saw the rooms priced at $300 two hours later than the rooms from which it would take her twenty minutes to get to work.

3. The rooms at Keats Court are more expensive than those she saw first, but not as expensive as those from which it would take thirty minutes to get to work.

4. Roberta saw the rooms in Milton Place earlier than those in Shelley Avenue, but later than the rooms where the rent was cheapest.

	Seen At				Rent				Work (minutes)			
	2:00 P.M.	3:00 P.M.	4:00 P.M.	5:00 P.M.	$200	$250	$300	$350	15	20	25	30
Byron Drive												
Keats Court												
Milton Place												
Shelley Avenue												
15 minutes									
20 minutes									
25 minutes									
30 minutes									
$200					
$250					
$300					
$350					

Address	Seen At	Rent	Work

Fruit for Lunch

In an effort to improve their daily intake of fresh fruit, four women each decided to have three different pieces of fruit for lunch today, choosing from an apple, a banana, an orange, or a pear. What was the order in which each woman ate her fruit, given that none chose to eat any fruit in the same order as anyone else?

1. The woman who ate an orange third also ate an apple directly before the order in which an apple was eaten by the woman who ate a pear first for lunch today.

2. Claire (who didn't eat an apple at all today) ate an orange directly before the order in which Teresa ate a banana.

3. The woman who ate an orange second didn't eat a banana today.

4. Stephanie ate a pear in an earlier order than Laura ate an apple.

	First				Second				Third			
	Apple	Banana	Orange	Pear	Apple	Banana	Orange	Pear	Apple	Banana	Orange	Pear
Claire												
Laura												
Stephanie												
Teresa												
Third Apple												
Banana												
Orange												
Pear												
Second Apple												
Banana												
Orange												
Pear												

Woman	First	Second	Third

Round the Table

Five pupils are seated at a table doing their homework, each assignment being in a different subject (as you would expect with a logic puzzle!). Study the clues to determine the occupant of each seat as depicted in the diagram below, together with his or her subject. (Note—Reference in the clues to "clockwise" does not necessarily mean starting from seat A.)

1. Looking clockwise around the table, we see: Cathy (who isn't studying biology); the student whose subject is geography; a student whose hair is shorter than Cathy's hair; the student whose subject is chemistry; and Martine.

2. Looking clockwise around the table, we see: Pauline (who isn't in seat A); the student whose subject is history; a student who is taller than the person in seat E; a student who is three months younger than the person in seat E; and Samuel (who isn't in seat C).

	Cathy	David	Martine	Pauline	Samuel	Biology	Chemistry	Geography	History	Mathematics
Seat A										
Seat B										
Seat C										
Seat D										
Seat E										
Biology										
Chemistry										
Geography										
History										
Mathematics										

Seat	Pupil	Subject

Long-distance Learners

When five new executives joined a company based in Colorado, they were asked to spend one month at the company's offices in Alaska and one month at the company's offices in Florida, to gain experience. The visits all took place in the same year, and no executive went to the same state in the same month as any other executive. Find out when they all visited Alaska and Florida by traveling through the clues.

1. The person who went to Florida in May traveled to Alaska either two months earlier or two months later than Alice's trip to Alaska.

2. The executive who traveled to Florida in March visited Alaska either three months earlier or three months later than Tony's trip to Alaska.

3. Peter's trip to Florida was earlier in the year than his trip to Alaska; and Peter's trip to Alaska was either two months earlier or two months later than Tony's trip to Florida. Tony's trip to Florida was neither the month before nor the month after Alice's trip to Florida.

4. September's trip to Florida was made by an executive who traveled to Alaska later in the year than Alice's trip to Alaska.

5. Naomi went to Florida four months after she made the trip to Alaska.

| | \multicolumn{5}{c}{Alaska} | \multicolumn{5}{c}{Florida} |
	January	March	April	July	September	February	March	May	August	September
Alice										
Michael										
Naomi										
Peter										
Tony										
February										
March										
May										
August										
September										

Florida

Executive	Alaska	Florida

Escape from Reality

Four women who are close friends share a hobby: each joined a virtual reality Web site on the Internet last year, and every evening the four women play out their fantasy lives, with a different name and occupation to those they have in the real world. See if you can work out who is whom, by day and by night!

1. Molly's avatar (virtual person) has a name that begins with the same letter as that of the real name of the woman (not Molly) who works as a casino dealer in the virtual world.

2. The woman who works as a cook at a local college enjoys her role as a model in the virtual world. The woman known as Francine works as an industrial spy when she goes online!

3. Anne drives taxis during the day. Her avatar has a name that begins with the same letter as that of the real name of the woman (not Freda) who calls herself Melissa in the virtual world.

	Job				Avatar's Name				Avatar's Job			
	Cook	Driver	Nurse	Teacher	Amanda	Francine	Melissa	Stella	Beautician	Dealer	Model	Spy
Anne												
Freda												
Molly												
Sue												
Avatar's Job Beautician												
Avatar's Job Dealer												
Avatar's Job Model												
Avatar's Job Spy												
Avatar's Name Amanda												
Avatar's Name Francine												
Avatar's Name Melissa												
Avatar's Name Stella												

4. The woman who calls herself Amanda when in her fantasy role works as a teacher during the day, but not as a beautician when online.

Player		Avatar	
Name	Job	Name	Job

pocket posh® christmas
logic 2

SOLUTIONS

1

Glenda is 17 (clue 4). The 20-year-old isn't Fran (clue 1), so Claire (3), and Debbie is 19. Thus Fran is 18 , and (1) Keith's girlfriend is Debbie. Debbie received two more cards than Claire (3), so Claire is George's girlfriend (2). Fran's boyfriend isn't Arthur (1), so Johnnie. Arthur's girlfriend is thus Glenda. The woman who received 12 cards isn't Claire (3), Glenda (4), or Fran (5), so Debbie, and (3) Claire received 10. Johnnie sent 6 cards (5), and Arthur sent 8 cards.

Thus:

Arthur - Glenda - 17 years
old - 8 cards;
George - Claire - 20 years old -
10 cards;
Johnnie - Fran - 18 years old - 6 cards;
Keith - Debbie - 19 years
old - 12 cards.

2

Remember throughout that each full name and address starts with three different letters (intro). The woman who lives on High Hill thus isn't Ms. Holt. Nor is her surname Vanderbilt (clue 1), Roberts (clue 2), or Aston (clue 3), so Ms. Lever lives on High Hill. The woman on Vale View isn't surnamed Vanderbilt (intro), Roberts (2), or Aston (3), so Holt. She isn't Heidi (intro), and Heidi doesn't live on High Hill, so she isn't surnamed Lever. Veronica's surname is Roberts (2). Heidi's isn't Vanderbilt (1), so Aston. Laura's surname isn't Lever (intro), so she doesn't live on High Hill (above). Heidi Aston doesn't live on Apple Avenue (intro), so either Low Lane or Rail Road, and (3) Laura lives on Vale View (Holt, above). Thus Rachel lives on Apple Avenue (4), and (by elimination) her surname is Vanderbilt. By elimination, Angela's surname is Lever. Veronica Roberts doesn't live on Rail Road (intro), so on Low Lane. Heidi lives on Rail Road.

Thus:

Angela - Lever - High Hill;
Heidi - Aston - Rail Road;
Laura - Holt - Vale View;
Rachel - Vanderbilt - Apple Avenue;
Veronica - Roberts - Low Lane.

3

Car E didn't have a collision on Maple Road (clue 1), Edge Avenue (clue 2), Forest Road (3), or Sycamore Drive (4), so Oxford Street. Thus car D was damaged on Edge Avenue (2), and car C hit a bus. Car A didn't hit a truck (1), a tree (3), or a wall (4), so a traffic sign. Car B didn't hit a tree (3), or a wall (4), so a truck and (1) car A had an accident on Maple Road. Car D (Edge Avenue, above) didn't hit a wall (2), so E hit a wall and D hit a tree. C wasn't on Forest Road (3), so Sycamore Drive. Car B was on Forest Road.

Thus:

Car A - traffic sign - Maple Road;
Car B - truck - Forest Road;
Car C - bus - Sycamore Drive;
Car D - tree - Edge Avenue;
Car E - wall - Oxford Street.

4

Stella made cookies (clue 2). No woman arrived sixth (grid). Natalie arrived fifth and didn't make donuts (clue 3), or a cake (seventh or eighth to arrive, 1), so scones. The cake wasn't made by Kathy (1), so Pam, and Kathy made donuts. The woman who arrived ninth wasn't Pam (1), or Stella (2), so Kathy. Pam was eighth (2), so Stella arrived seventh. The woman who spent $25 wasn't Stella (2), or Natalie (3), so Pam (1), and Kathy spent $30. Stella didn't spend $40 (2), so $35. Natalie spent $40.

Thus:

Kathy - ninth - donuts - $30;
Natalie - fifth - scones - $40;
Pam - eighth - cake - $25;
Stella - seventh - cookies - $35.

5

Micky lives in The Moorings (clue 3), so (clue 1) Helen lives in Amber Hill. The person whose bus left at 5:05 P.M. isn't Helen (4), or Andrew (5), so Micky (3), and Sue's left at 5:08 P.M. Helen's left at 5:15 P.M. (4), and Andrew's at 5:12 P.M. Sue (5:08 P.M. departure, above) doesn't live in Lakeside (2), so Wood Lodge and Andrew lives in Lakeside. The No. 16 bus wasn't taken by Andrew or Helen (5), or Sue (2), so by Micky. Sue didn't take the No. 87 (3), so the No. 42 (2), and Andrew took the No. 24. Helen took the No. 87.

Thus:

Andrew - Lakeside - No. 24 - 5:12 P.M.;
Helen - Amber Hill - No. 87 - 5:15 P.M.;
Micky - The Moorings - No. 16 - 5:05 P.M.;
Sue - Wood Lodge - No. 42 - 5:08 P.M.

6

The watch was from Lynda's father (clue 2), and the book was from her grandma (clue 3). The teddy bear wasn't from her brother or sister (1), so her mother. The present containing a doll was opened fifth (4), so wasn't from her brother (1). Thus her sister gave the doll and her brother gave the kite. The first present opened wasn't from her brother (1), mother or grandma (3), so her father. The present opened second wasn't from her brother (1), so her mother (3), and the one from her grandma was opened third. The present from Lynda's brother was opened fourth.

Thus:
Brother - kite - fourth;
Father - watch - first;
Grandma - book - third;
Mother - teddy bear - second;
Sister - doll - fifth.

7

The art book is either A or D (clue 1), and the books with blue and yellow covers are either B and/or C. Thus the fishing book with a red cover is E (clue 3), and book A is on sport and (by elimination) has a brown cover. Thus D has a green cover and is on art, C is blue (1), and B is yellow. C is on wild flowers (2), so B is on birds.

Thus:
Book A - brown - sport;
Book B - yellow - birds;
Book C - blue - wild flowers;
Book D - green - art;
Book E - red - fishing.

8

Danny wasn't married in December (clue 1), so the wedding in Barbados was in June (clue 3), Danny married in September and the March wedding was in Sardinia. Sarah's husband isn't Stuart (1), or Danny (September, above). Julia's husband is Carl (2), so Sarah's is Mike. Deirdre isn't married to Danny (1), so Danny married Maria and Deirdre married Stuart. Julia didn't marry in June (1), or December (2), so March. Deirdre didn't marry

in December (1), so June, and Sarah married in December. Maria married in Majorca (4), so Sarah's wedding was in Tenerife.

Thus:
Deirdre - Stuart - Barbados - June;
Julia - Carl - Sardinia - March;
Maria - Danny - Majorca - September;
Sarah - Mike - Tenerife - December.

9

The man with 9 nieces and 6 nephews isn't Mr. Grainger (clue 4), Mr. Venner (clue 1), or Mr. Harte (2), so Mr. Thorpe. He isn't Patrick (1), Ronnie (1), or Norman (3), so Theo. By elimination, Norman has 7 nieces and 5 nephews (3), so Patrick has 8 nieces and 7 nephews (1), thus Ronnie has 6 nieces and 8 nephews. Patrick is Mr. Harte (2). Norman isn't Mr. Venner (1), so his surname is Grainger and Ronnie's is Venner.

Thus (nieces - nephews):
Norman - Grainger - 7 - 5;
Patrick - Harte - 8 - 7;
Ronnie - Venner - 6 - 8;
Theo - Thorpe - 9 - 6.

10

The boy who hit a cyclist wore a red hat (clue 1), the one who hit a dog wore a green hat (clue 3), and Martin hit a car (4). Simon in the blue hat (2) didn't hit a neighbor, so a window. William's hat is purple (5), so (by elimination), he hit a neighbor. By elimination, Martin's hat is cream. Larry's hat isn't green (3), so red, and Andy's is green.

Thus:

Andy - green - dog;
Larry - red - cyclist;
Martin - cream - car;
Simon - blue - window;
William - purple - neighbor.

11

Ben wrote the music for "Single Girl" (clue 1), and Tania wrote the music for "No Thoughts" (clue 3), Suzi wrote the music and Tania wrote the words for one song (2), so the person who wrote the music to go with James's words for "Stay Free" (1) is Will. Suzi's music and Tania's words don't feature on "Why Not?" (2), so "Fast Mover." By elimination, James wrote the music for "Why Not?". The words to "Why Not?" weren't written by Will (2), or Ben (4), so Suzi. By elimination, Ben wrote the words for "No Thoughts" and Will wrote the words for "Single Girl".

Thus (words - music):

"Fast Mover "- Tania - Suzi;
"No Thoughts" - Ben - Tania;
"Single Girl" - Will - Ben;
"Stay Free" - James - Will;
"Why Not?" - Suzi - James.

12

Liam Pearce's stage name is Dave Darnley (clue 3). Kevin Marsh's stage name isn't Arthur Ayr (clue 1), or Clarke Crowe (2), so Bill Benson. Man A isn't Arthur Ayr (1), Dave Darnley (3), or Bill Benson (5), so Clark Crowe. Kevin Marsh/Bill Benson didn't appear in The Pirate (1), Wise Choice (2), or Dead Calm (5), so Fortunate. He isn't B or C (4), so D. Arthur Ayr is C (1), and the star of The Pirate is B. By elimination, Dave Darnley is B. Man A wasn't in Wise Choice (2), so Dead Calm, and C was in Wise Choice. Man A is Tom Watson (3), so C is Bert Cox.

Thus:

Man A - Clark Crowe - Tom Watson - Dead Calm;
Man B - Dave Darnley - Liam Pearce - The Pirate;
Man C - Arthur Ayr - Bert Cox - Wise Choice;
Man D - Bill Benson - Kevin Marsh - Fortunate.

13

The player who made NOT isn't Adam (clue 1), Lorna (clue 2), or Jill (3), so Pete, whose 5-letter word was thus LOUSE (4). LIT wasn't Lorna's (2), or Jill's (3), so Adam's, and (1) Pete's 4-letter word was ROSE. Lorna didn't make NOTE or TILE (2), so LOSE. Her 5-letter word wasn't OUTER or STONE (2), so ROUSE. Adam's wasn't STONE (5), so OUTER and Jill's was STONE. Adam didn't make TILE (2), so NOTE. Jill thus made TILE, but not ORE (2), so SIN. Lorna's 3-letter word was ORE.

Thus:

Adam - LIT - NOTE - OUTER;
Jill - SIN - TILE - STONE;
Lorna - ORE - LOSE - ROUSE;
Pete - NOT - ROSE - LOUSE.

14

Mr. Farmer teaches geography (clue 2), and Mr. Gould was the salesperson (clue 4). The former musician who now teaches music isn't Mrs. Elliott (1), or Miss Cross (3), so Mr. Dawson. The former acrobat who now teaches biology isn't Miss Cross, so Mrs. Elliott. Mr. Farmer wasn't a clerk (2), so a bar manager. Miss Cross was a clerk (3). She doesn't teach English (3), so history. Mr. Gould teaches English.

Thus:

Miss Cross - clerk - history;
Mr. Dawson - musician - music;
Mrs. Elliott - acrobat - biology;
Mr. Farmer - bar
 manager - geography;
Mr. Gould - salesperson - English.

15

Remember throughout that each person's first name, surname, and birthday month begin with three

different letters (intro), thus the person surnamed Jones wasn't born in July, so (clue 3) either May or September, and Stephen was born in July. Marjorie's surname is Oldman (clue 4). Stephen's isn't Saunders (intro), or Allen (1), so Major. Arnold's birthday isn't in April (intro), so May (2). He isn't surnamed Allen (intro), so Owen is Allen (1), and Jenny (not Jones, intro) is surnamed Saunders. By elimination, Arnold's surname is Jones. Owen's birthday isn't in October (intro), so Jenny's is in October and Owen's is in September. Marjorie's birthday is in April.

Thus:

Arnold - Jones - May;
Jenny - Saunders - October;
Marjorie - Oldman - April;
Owen - Allen - September;
Stephen - Major - July.

16

The person who spent 2½ hours in the library isn't Judy (clue 2), Lionel, or Trish (clue 3), so Martin. The one who spent 3 hours in the library isn't Judy (2), so Trish (3), and Lionel was there for 3½ hours. Judy was there for 4 hours, so Trish studied politics. Judy studied coins (2). Martin arrived at 9:00 A.M. (3), so he studied butterflies (1), and Lionel arrived at 9:30 A.M. and studied flags. Trish arrived at 9:15 A.M. (2), and Judy at 8:45 A.M.

Thus:

Judy - 8:45 A.M. - 4 hours - coins;
Lionel - 9:30 A.M. - 3½ hours - flags;
Martin - 9:00 A.M. - 2½ hours - butterflies;
Trish - 9:15 A.M. - 3 hours - politics.

17

Monday's event wasn't the snowboard or skating competition (clue 2), or the ski jump (clue 3), so the toboggan race. Thursday's event won by Wilhelm wasn't the ski jump (3), or snowboard (2), so skating. The snowboarding contest wasn't won by Max (1), or Anton (2), so George. Max didn't win on Monday (1), so his event was the ski jump and Anton's was the toboggan race. The snowboard event was at location B (1). Location A wasn't the site of the toboggan race (1), or skating competition (3), so the ski jump. The snowboard event was on Wednesday (4), and Thursday's event was at site D. Thus the ski jump was on Tuesday and the toboggan event was at site C.

Thus:

Skating - D - Wilhelm - Thursday;
Ski jump - A - Max - Tuesday;
Snowboard - B - George - Wednesday;
Toboggan - C - Anton - Monday.

18

The man who got 160 doubloons wasn't Dirty Dave (clue 1), Horrible Hugh, or Nasty Ned (clue 2), or Sly Sam (3), so Evil Edmund. No one got 130 ducats (grid), so the man who got 120 ducats wasn't Dirty Dave, or Evil Edmund (1), Horrible Hugh, or Sly Sam (2). Thus Nasty Ned got 120 ducats and (3) Sly Sam got 150 ducats. Dirty Dave got 170 (1), and Evil Edmund got 160 ducats, so Horrible Hugh got 140 ducats. Dirty Dave got 140 doubloons (1). Horrible Hugh got more doubloons than Nasty Ned (2) who got more than Sly Sam (3), so Horrible Hugh got 150, Nasty Ned got 130, and Sly Sam got 120 doubloons.

Thus (doubloons - ducats):

Dirty Dave - 140 - 170;
Evil Edmund - 160 - 160;
Horrible Hugh - 150 - 140;
Nasty Ned - 130 - 120;
Sly Sam - 120 - 150.

19

Lena May has turquoise sails (clue 3), so in clue 1, it's between the yacht with the white sails and *West Wind*; and in clue 2, it's between *Ariadne* and the yacht with red sails. The latter isn't in position D (2), so *Lena May* isn't yacht C. The yacht with orange sails isn't B (1), so *West Wind* isn't A, and *Lena May* isn't E. *Lena May* isn't B or D (3), so A. Thus B is *West*

Wind (1), C has orange sails, D is *Tamarind*, and E has white sails. B has red sails (2), C is *Skipper*, D has yellow sails, and E is *Ariadne*.

Thus:

Yacht A - *Lena May* - turquoise;
Yacht B - *West Wind* - red;
Yacht C - *Skipper* - orange;
Yacht D - *Tamarind* - yellow;
Yacht E - *Ariadne* - white.

20

The Mercedes finished either first or second (clue 2), as did the Jaguar (clue 3), thus Mr. Bishop drove neither the Mercedes or the Jaguar (2). Mr. Bishop didn't drive the Porsche (1), so the Ferrari. By elimination, Mr. Davis drove the Porsche (3). Terry is neither Mr. Bishop nor Mr. Davis (1), so Terry finished second, Mr. Davis was third and Mr. Bishop was fourth. The Jaguar was first (3). Benjamin wasn't first, second or third (3), so fourth and (4) Harry was third. By elimination, Keith was first and Terry drove the Mercedes. Keith's surname isn't Exbury (5), so Colt, and Terry's is Exbury.

Thus:

Benjamin - Bishop - Ferrari - fourth;
Harry - Davis - Porsche - third;
Keith - Colt - Jaguar - first;
Terry - Exbury - Mercedes - second.

21

The 2007 winner wasn't *Sad Souls* (clue 2), or *Bella's Tale* (clue 3). If *True Devotion* won in 2007, then Ms. Dale won in 2006 (1), leaving no possible years for Ms. Hart's *No Return* (3). So the 2007 winner was *No Return* and (3) *Bella's Tale* won in 2005. Ms. Dale wrote *Bella's Tale* (1), and *True Devotion* won in 2006. Thus *Sad Souls* won in 2004. Lara won in 2005 (2), and Amelia in 2006. Maggie's surname is Maughan (4), so (by elimination) she won in 2004, Amelia's surname is Bennett, and Sheila won in 2007.

Thus:

2004 - *Sad Souls* - Maggie - Maughan;
2005 - *Bella's Tale* - Lara - Dale;
2006 - *True Devotion* - Amelia - Bennett;
2007 - *No Return* - Sheila - Hart.

22

Monday's program featured the hockey player (clue 2). Friday's didn't feature the supermodel (clue 1), or the comedian (3), so the singer (4), and Thursday's featured the magician. The snake pit trial involved the supermodel (1), so the comedian appeared on Wednesday's program (3), and Thursday's trial involved the icy bath. By elimination, Tuesday's program featured the supermodel.

The comedian thus took part in the climbing trial (1). Grub-eating wasn't the hockey player's trial (2), so the singer's. The hockey player took part in the tank of eels trial.

Thus:

Comedian - Wednesday - climbing;
Hockey
    player - Monday - tank of eels;
Magician - Thursday - icy bath;
Singer - Friday - grub-eating;
Supermodel - Tuesday - snake pit.

23

The person with the 10-minute (shortest) delay wasn't Mrs. Barton (clue 2), Mr. Walters (clue 3), Mr. Price or Miss Scott (4), so Mr. King, and (2) Mrs. Barton had the 12-minute delay. The person with the 14-minute delay wasn't Mr. Walters (3), or Mr. Price (4), so Miss Scott. The electricity company's construction didn't affect Mrs. Barton (3), so Mr. King, and Mr. Walters had a 16-minute delay. By elimination, Mr. Price was delayed for 18 minutes. Mrs. Barton's delay wasn't caused by the telephone (1), gas, or line painting companies (2), so by the water company. The telephone company's construction caused the 18-minute delay (1), and the gas company's caused the 14-minute delay, so the line painting company's construction caused a delay of 16 minutes.

Thus:

Electricity - Mr. King - 10 minutes;
Gas - Miss Scott - 14 minutes;
Line painting - Mr. Walters -
    16 minutes;
Telephone - Mr. Price - 18 minutes;
Water - Mrs. Barton - 12 minutes.

24

Vincent works on Fridays (clue 3). The person who works on Monday isn't Sally (clue 2), or Jane (4), so Ken and (1) the person who works on Wednesday has traded for 10 years. The latter isn't Sally (5), so Jane. Sally works on Tuesday. Vincent sells pottery (4). Ken sells fruit (2), and (5) has traded for 8 years. Thus Vincent has traded for 5 years (3), and Jane is the bookseller. Sally sells flowers and has traded for 4 years.

Thus:

Jane - Wednesday - books - 10 years;
Ken - Monday- fruit - 8 years;
Sally - Tuesday - flowers - 4 years;
Vincent - Friday - pottery - 5 years.

25

The men holding the ace and/or 3 of spades aren't Simon (clue 3), or Damian (clue 4). Henry hasn't the ace of spades (1), so he has the 3 and George has the ace. The man with the 7 of hearts has the 3 of clubs (1), and either the 5 or jack of spades, so isn't George (above). Damian has the 5 of spades (2), and Henry has the queen of clubs. By elimination, Simon has the jack of spades. Damian has the 3 of clubs (3). Simon has the 4 of hearts. Simon has the 7 of clubs (3), and George has the 5 of clubs. Henry has the king of hearts (6), and George has the 9 of hearts.

Thus (club - heart - spade):
Damian - 3 - 7 - 5;
George - 5 - 9 - A;
Henry - Q - K - 3;
Simon - 7 - 4 - J.

26

Friday's meeting isn't of the guitar or swimming clubs (clue 1), drama club (clue 2), or bird-watching club (3), so the table tennis club, and (4) Bob's club meets on Thursday. Monday's isn't attended by Darren (1), William (2), or Poppy (3), so Lisa. Tuesday's isn't attended by Darren (1), or William (2), so Poppy (3), and the bird-watching club is on Monday. Darren's club isn't on Wednesday (1), so Friday. William's meets on Wednesday. Bob attends the swimming club (1). William doesn't go to the drama club (2), so the guitar club. Poppy attends the drama club.

Thus:
Bob - swimming - Thursday;
Darren - table tennis - Friday;
Lisa - bird-watching - Monday;
Poppy - drama - Tuesday;
William - guitar - Wednesday.

27

Remember throughout that each new picture contains pieces of three old ones (intro). Romeo's head is with Juliet's body (clue 2). Banquo's legs and Othello's body (clue 1) aren't with Juliet's head, so (by elimination) they're in the same picture as Desdemona's head. Juliet's legs aren't with Othello's head (3), so Banquo's. Romeo's body has Desdemona's legs (4) so (by elimination) Desdemona's body is with Juliet's legs, Romeo's legs are with Banquo's body, and Juliet's body is with Othello's legs. Romeo's body isn't with Juliet's head (4), so Othello's. Banquo's body has Juliet's head.

Thus (head - body - legs):
Banquo - Desdemona - Juliet;
Desdemona - Othello - Banquo;
Juliet - Banquo - Romeo;
Othello - Romeo - Desdemona;
Romeo - Juliet - Othello.

28

Brenda's news was her pregnancy (clue 1). Matthew's wasn't about graduation or a new home (clue 2), so his engagement. Matthew wrote the letter (2). Tuesday's news was told in person, but not by Brenda or Jeff (3), so Tina. The e-mail wasn't sent by Brenda or Tina (1), so by Jeff. By elimination, Brenda made the phone call. Jeff's news wasn't of the graduation (1), so a new home, and Tina's was of the graduation. The e-mail came on Wednesday (1). The phone call wasn't made on Friday (3), so Thursday. Friday's news came by letter.

Thus:

Tuesday - in person - Tina - graduation;
Wednesday - e-mail - Jeff - new home;
Thursday - phone call - Brenda - pregnancy;
Friday - letter - Matthew - engagement.

29

No. 7 is red (clue 1). The blue drawers (clue 2) are either No. 2 or No. 3 in the top row, either No. 5 or No. 6 in the middle and either No. 11 or No. 12 in the bottom row. No. 8 is of the same color as No. 11 (1), so not blue (above), Thus No. 12 is blue. No. 5 isn't blue (4), so No. 6 is blue, as is No. 3 (3). No. 5 isn't yellow (5), so green, and No. 8 is yellow, as is No. 11 (1). The yellow drawer in the top row isn't No. 4 (2), or No. 2 (5), so No. 1. No. 4 and No. 9 aren't red (2), so green. No. 2 and No. 10 are red.

Thus (top - middle - bottom):

Blue - 3 - 6 - 12;
Green - 4 - 5 - 9;
Red - 2 - 7 - 10;
Yellow - 1 - 8 - 11.

30

The man whose face is on the $3 stamp came to power in either 1990 or 1994 (clue 2), and the $6 stamp features Zog, who came to power in 1994 or 1998. So Zug, who came to power in 1988 (clue 3), features on the $5 stamp and the $4 stamp shows the man who came to power in 1996. Zag features on the $4 stamp (1), and the $2 stamp features the man who came to power four years before Zeg. Thus (by elimination) the $2 stamp features Zig who came to power in 1990, Zeg came to power in 1994 (2), and Zog in 1998.

Thus:

Zag - 1996 - $4;
Zeg - 1994 - $3;
Zig - 1990 - $2;
Zog - 1998 - $6;
Zug - 1988 - $5.

31

The house seen at 12:15 P.M. was too isolated (clue 4), so the house which was too small was seen at 11:30 A.M. (1), and Thursday's viewing was at 10:45 A.M. Friday's appointment wasn't at 11:30 A.M. or 10:15 A.M. (3), or 12:15 P.M. (4), so 12:45 P.M. Either the 11:30 A.M. viewing was on Wednesday and the 10:15 A.M. viewing was on Tuesday (3), or the 11:30 A.M. viewing was on Tuesday and the 10:15 A.M. viewing was on Monday. In other words, Tuesday's viewing was at either 10:15 A.M. or 11:30 A.M. The house seen on Monday was too noisy (2), so (by elimination) the 12:15 P.M. viewing was on Wednesday. So Monday's was at 10:15 A.M. (3), and Tuesday's at 11:30 A.M. The house seen on Thursday was too cold (4), so the house seen on Friday was too damp.

Thus:

Monday - 10:15 A.M. - too noisy;
Tuesday - 11:30 A.M. - too small;
Wednesday - 12:15 P.M. -
   too isolated;
Thursday - 10:45 A.M. - too cold;
Friday - 12:45 P.M. - too damp.

32

The woman at No. 1 doesn't prefer wildlife (clue 1), travel (clue 2), or sports (3), so crime. Her surname isn't Derby (2), Vance (3), or Edwards (4), so Rigden. The wildlife enthusiast lives at No. 2 (1), and Sheila at No. 3. Helen who prefers sports lives at No. 4 (3). By elimination, Sheila's favorite is travel, so (2) Paula is Mrs. Derby and lives at No. 2; and Jean is Mrs. Rigden. Sheila's surname isn't Vance (1), so Edwards. Helen's surname is Vance.

Thus:

Helen - Vance - No. 4 - sports;
Jean - Rigden - No. 1 - crime;
Paula - Derby - No. 2 - wildlife;
Sheila - Edwards - No. 3 - travel.

33

Remember throughout that each man's role, description, first name and surname begin with four different letters (clue 1). Bayliss is the drunkard (clue 4). The cop isn't Daly (3), so Pritchard, who isn't played by the actor surnamed Davies (2), so Brown. Pritchard isn't played by Chester (2), so by Dave. By elimination, Coren is either the burglar or the painter, played by either Bob or Peter, so the man who plays him has the only remaining initial, D, for his surname—thus he's Mr. Davies. He isn't the painter (2), so the burglar and (by elimination) the actor playing him is Peter. Bayliss is thus played by Chester and Daly is played by Bob. Daly is the painter. Chester's surname is Pryce and Bob's is Crouch.

Thus:

Bayliss - drunkard - Chester - Pryce;
Coren - burglar - Peter - Davies;
Daly - painter - Bob - Crouch;
Pritchard - cop - Dave - Brown.

34

Mr. Yates had a head injury (clue 4). No one was away for 7 days (grid). The person away for 4 days with a sore throat (clue 1) isn't Mr. Chester or Miss Bourn (2), or Mrs. Hudson (3), so Mr. Newton. Mrs. Hudson didn't have a sprained ankle or a stomach bug (3), so a cough. She wasn't away for 9 days (3), so the person with a stomach bug wasn't away for 8 or 9 days. Mr. Chester was away for 8 or 9 days (2), so (by elimination) he had a sprained ankle and Miss Bourn had a stomach bug. The person away for 5 days isn't Mrs. Hudson (3), or Mr. Yates (4), so Miss Bourn, and (2) Mr. Chester was away for 8 days. Thus Mrs. Hudson was away for 6 days (3), and Mr. Yates for 9 days.

Thus:

Miss Bourn - 5 days - stomach bug;
Mr. Chester - 8
    days - sprained ankle;
Mrs. Hudson - 6 days - cough;
Mr. Newton - 4 days - sore throat;
Mr. Yates - 9 days - head injury.

35

Norah recommended the gardener (clue 2), and Dora recommended the carpenter (clue 4). Laura didn't recommend the electrician or the plumber (1), so the decorator. The decorator's card isn't No. 1 (3), so No. 3 (1), and the electrician's card is No. 5. Flora gave No. 2 (3). By elimination, Cora gave No. 5 and Flora gave the plumber's card. Norah didn't give No. 4 (2), so No. 1. Dora gave No. 4.

Thus:

Cora - electrician - No. 5;
Dora - carpenter - No. 4;
Flora - plumber - No. 2;
Laura - decorator - No. 3;
Norah - gardener - No. 1.

36

Thelma's first, second and third choices didn't include Munchies (clue 2), so Julie, Louisa, and Sandy all rated Munchies in some order. Sandy chose Crunchies second (clue 3), so not Munchies third (2). Thus her rating of Munchies was in first place. The woman who chose Chockies second and Munchies third (2) wasn't Thelma, so Thelma chose Flakies second. The woman who chose Flakies first wasn't Julie (1), so Louisa. The one who rated Flakies third wasn't Julie (1), so Sandy. Louisa's second choice wasn't Chockies (3), so Munchies and (1) Julie rated Munchies third. By elimination, Julie's first choice was Crunchies, so Thelma's first was Chockies. Thus Thelma's third was Crunchies and Louisa's third was Chockies.

Thus (first - second - third):

Julie - Crunchies - Chockies - Munchies;
Louisa - Flakies - Munchies - Chockies;
Sandy - Munchies - Crunchies - Flakies;
Thelma - Chockies - Flakies - Crunchies.

37

Desmond ordered sorbet (clue 1). Eileen didn't order cheesecake (clue 3). Nor, because she received ice cream (3), did she order ice cream. Thus Eileen ordered apple pie. So Gina's table number was one higher than Eileen's (2), thus

Gina didn't order cheesecake (3). By elimination, Gina ordered ice cream and Frederick ordered cheesecake. Table 4 wasn't taken by Gina (2), Frederick or Eileen (3 and above), so Desmond. Frederick had table 1, Eileen had table 2 (3), and Gina had table 3 (2). Desmond received apple pie (2). Frederick's order of cheesecake was thus received by Gina. Frederick received the sorbet.

Thus (ordered - received):
Desmond - table 4 - sorbet - apple pie;
Eileen - table 2 - apple pie - ice cream;
Frederick - table 1 - cheesecake - sorbet;
Gina - table 3 - ice cream - cheesecake.

38

Hope was cooking in the afternoon (clue 2), and Charity was gardening in the morning (clue 3). The woman who did the cleaning in the morning and laundry in the afternoon isn't Faith or Constance (1), so Joy. Thus Hope did the laundry in the morning. The woman who did the gardening in the afternoon wasn't Charity (gardening in the morning), or Constance (1), so Faith. Faith's morning job was the same as Constance's afternoon job (1), so shopping. Charity did the cleaning in the afternoon and Constance did the cooking in the morning.

Thus (morning - afternoon):
Charity - gardening - cleaning;
Constance - cooking - shopping;
Faith - shopping - gardening;
Hope - laundry - cooking;
Joy - cleaning - laundry.

39

The person in car D was writing (clue 3), so cars A and/or B belong to Patricia who was knitting (clue 1), and a *man* who was singing. That man wasn't Malcolm (2), so Richard. Beth drove car D (2), and Malcolm was in E. Richard was thus in A (2), and Patricia was in B. By elimination, Judy was in C. She wasn't phoning (4), so reading. Malcolm was phoning.

Thus:
Car A - Richard - singing;
Car B - Patricia - knitting;
Car C - Judy - reading;
Car D - Beth - writing;
Car E - Malcolm - phoning.

40

The shop opening on the 29th isn't in Fort George (clue 1), Brookford (clue 2), or Windridge (3), so Netherton. Mitchell's sells shoes and opens on the 23rd (4). The shop that opens on the 11th isn't The Zone (2), or Fifteen (3), so Dean & Co. The Zone isn't opening on the 17th (2), so the 29th. Thus Fifteen will open on the 17th and (3) Dean & Co is in Windridge. The toy shop opens six days after the shop in Fort George (1), so The Zone sells toys, Mitchell's is in Fort George and Fifteen is in Brookford. Dean & Co sells clothes (2), so Fifteen sells books.

Thus:

Dean & Co - Windridge - clothes - 11th;
Fifteen - Brookford - books - 17th;
Mitchell's - Fort George - shoes - 23rd;
The Zone - Netherton - toys - 29th.

41

The man whose baby is due in April isn't David (clue 1), Jerry (clue 2), or Sam (3), so Colin. The baby due in March isn't David's (1), or Sam's (3), so Jerry's. Thus Colin craves cheese (2). He isn't married to Debbie (1), Martine (2), or Ruth (4), so Caroline. Ruth's baby is due in January (4), and Sam's in February, so Ruth is married to David. Debbie's husband craves prawns (1), and Sam craves salmon (3), so Debbie is married to Jerry and Martine to Sam. By elimination, Ruth's husband craves bacon.

Thus:

Caroline - Colin - April - cheese;
Debbie - Jerry - March - prawns;
Martine - Sam - February - salmon;
Ruth - David - January - bacon.

42

Mrs. Stoker's new number isn't 54 (clue 5), so either 61 or 65 (clue 3), and Mr. Mason's new number is either 65 or 69. Mr. Havelock's new number isn't 54, 58, or 65 (4). No old apartment has a number with digits totaling 9, so Mr. White is the person at No. 58 (1), and he used to be at No. 49. By elimination, Miss Carter is at No. 54. Mr. Mason wasn't at No. 59 (2), so was at No. 51 (4), and Mr. Havelock's new number is 61. Thus Mr. Mason is at No. 69 (3), and Mrs. Stoker is at No. 65. Mrs. Stoker was at No. 59 (5), Mr. Havelock at No. 62 and Miss Carter at No. 43.

Thus (old - new):

Miss Carter - No. 43 - No. 54;
Mr. Havelock - No. 62 - No. 61;
Mr. Mason - No. 51 - No. 69;
Mrs. Stoker - No. 59 - No. 65;
Mr. White - No. 49 - No. 58.

43

The party on the 13th isn't Henry's (clue 1), Philip's (clue 2), Jack's (3), or Neil's (4), so Lionel's. Thus Neil's is on the 7th (4), and the emigration party is on the 11th. Neil's party isn't to celebrate retirement (1), graduation (2), or a birthday (3), so a book launch. Jack's party is on the 11th (3), and the birthday party is on the 13th. Henry's is on the 10th (1), and the retirement party is on the 9th. By elimination, Henry is holding the graduation party. Philip's is on the 9th (2), so the emigration party is Jack's.

Thus:

Henry - graduation - 10th;
Jack - emigration - 11th;
Lionel - birthday - 13th;
Neil - book launch - 7th;
Philip - retirement - 9th.

44

Remember throughout that each man has three different quantities (intro). Thus the man with 7 old shirts has 10 odd socks (clue 2), and Fred has 9 odd socks. The man with 6 odd socks has 8 old shirts (1), and Tony has 9 old shirts, so (by elimination) Tony also has 7 odd socks and Fred has 5 old shirts. Thus Fred (9 odd socks, above) has 10 torn pairs of pants (1), and Tony has 11 torn pairs of pants. The man with 8 old shirts has 9 torn pairs of pants and the one with 8 torn pairs of pants has 7 old shirts. Marty has 7 old shirts (3), and Vernon has 8 old shirts.

Thus (socks - shirts - pants):

Fred - 9 - 5 - 10;
Marty - 10 - 7 - 8;
Tony - 7 - 9 - 11;
Vernon - 6 - 8 - 9.

45

Remember throughout that each rumor involved three different women (intro). Alison talked about one woman flirting (clue 1). The rumor of laziness, which was about Chrissie, didn't involve Barbara (clue 2), so

Diane was the talker and Alison was the listener. Chrissie listened to the gambling rumor (3), so (by elimination) Barbara talked about Alison gambling. The rumor of flirting talked of by Alison (1) was thus about Diane (3). So Barbara listened to the flirting rumor and Diane listened to the drinking rumor. The drinking rumor was started by Chrissie and was about Barbara.

Thus (talker - listener - about):

Drinking - Chrissie - Diane - Barbara;
Flirting - Alison - Barbara - Diane;
Gambling - Barbara - Chrissie - Alison;
Laziness - Diane - Alison - Chrissie.

46

Remember throughout that each new picture contains pieces of three old ones (intro). The English teacher's head is with the geography teacher's body (clue 1), and the geography teacher's legs are with the French teacher's body (clue 2). The history teacher's head and science teacher's legs (3) are (by elimination) with the English teacher's body. By elimination the science teacher's head is with the French teacher's body. The French teacher's legs aren't with the geography teacher's head (4), so they're with the English teacher's head. By elimination, the science teacher's body is with the history teacher's legs, and the history teacher's body is with the English teacher's legs. The geography teacher's head isn't with the history teacher's body (4), so the science teacher's body. The French teacher's head has the history teacher's body.

Thus (head - body - legs):
English - geography - French;
French - history - English;
Geography - science - history;
History - English - science;
Science - French - geography.

47

Either the J.J. Forrester factory was built in 1882 and the one making lifeboats was built in 1886 (clue 2), or the J.J. Forrester factory was built in 1886 and the one making lifeboats was built in 1890. In other words, the 1886 factory was either of J.J. Forrester or made lifeboats. The factory built in 1882 made pumps (clue 3), so Arnott's, which made blocks and tackle, was in the 1892 building (1), and propellers were made in the 1890 building. Thus lifeboats were made in the 1886 building (2), and the 1882 building housed J.J. Forrester. By elimination, steam engines were made in the 1884 building. McDonald's wasn't in the 1884 building (4), so the 1884 building housed Seatrader, McDonald's was in the 1886 building and Dagg & Meek in the 1890 building.

Thus:
1882 - J.J. Forrester - pumps;
1884 - Seatrader - steam engines;
1886 - McDonald's - lifeboats;
1890 - Dagg & Meek - propellers;
1892 - Arnott's - blocks/tackle.

48

The priest at St. Mark's is Reverend Lane (clue 1). The man at St. Andrew's isn't Reverend Carter or Reverend Thomas (clue 2), so Reverend Walsh. The All Saints' priest held an auction (3), so Reverend Thomas who organized the three-legged race (2) is priest at St. Mary's and Reverend Carter is at All Saints'. The church sale wasn't at St. Mark's (1), so St. Andrew's. The dance was at St. Mark's. The priest of All Saints' raised $1,700 (3). The priest who raised $1,300 isn't at St. Andrew's (1), or St. Mary's (2), so St. Mark's. The man who raised $1,900 isn't at St. Andrew's (2), so St. Mary's. Thus $1,500 was raised at St. Andrew's.

Thus:
All Saints' - Reverend Carter - auction - $1,700;
St. Andrew's - Reverend Walsh - church sale - $1,500;
St. Mark's - Reverend Lane - dance - $1,300;
St. Mary's - Reverend Thomas - fun run - $1,900.

49

The person who took 11 clear bottles isn't Faith (clue 1), Gordon (clue 2), or Jane (3), so Kenneth who (4), thus took 10 brown bottles. Jane didn't take 6 green (3), so she didn't take 7 clear. The person who took 7 clear isn't Gordon (2), so Faith. The one who took 12 brown isn't Gordon (2), or Jane (3), so Faith. Gordon took 11 brown and 9 clear (2), so Jane took 8 brown, 8 clear, and (3) 7 green. Gordon took 6 green (2), so Kenneth took 8 (4), and Faith took 9 green bottles.

Thus:

Faith - 12 brown - 9 green - 7 clear;
Gordon - 11 brown - 6 green - 9 clear;
Jane - 8 brown - 7 green - 8 clear;
Kenneth - 10 brown - 8 green - 11 clear.

50

Remember throughout that each woman wore three different colors (intro). The woman with a green hat had a navy scarf (clue 4). The one with a red scarf didn't have a turquoise hat (clue 2), and the one with a turquoise hat didn't have a maroon scarf (3). So the one with a turquoise hat had a green scarf. The one with a maroon hat had a green coat (3). The one with a red scarf had either a maroon or navy hat, so (2) the one with a turquoise scarf had either a maroon or navy coat. Thus the woman with a green coat had a red scarf (2), and the one with a maroon coat had a turquoise scarf. The one in a red coat had a navy hat (1), and the one in a turquoise coat had a navy scarf. So the woman in a maroon coat had a red hat, the one in a navy coat had a turquoise hat and the one in a red coat had a maroon scarf.

Thus (coat - hat - scarf):

Green - maroon - red;
Maroon - red - turquoise;
Navy - turquoise - green;
Red - navy - maroon;
Turquoise - green - navy.

51

The 12:30 P.M. flight isn't to Oslo (clue 1), Gibraltar or Lisbon (clue 2), or Alicante (3), so Singapore, and (4) is being dealt with by Desk 4. The Desk 2 flight will thus depart at 1:15 P.M. (2), the Gibraltar flight at 1:45 P.M. and the flight to Lisbon at 2:00 P.M. The flight to Alicante departs at 1:00 P.M. (3), and that being dealt with at the desk next to it departs at 1:15 P.M. By elimination, the latter is to Oslo, so the flight to Alicante isn't being dealt with at desk 5. Desk 5 isn't dealing with passengers to Gibraltar (4), so Lisbon. Desk 1 isn't dealing with the 1:45 departure (5), so the Gibraltar flight (1:45 P.M., above) is dealt with by Desk 3 and the Alicante flight by Desk 1.

Thus:

Desk 1 - Alicante - 1:00 P.M.;
Desk 2 - Oslo - 1:15 P.M.;
Desk 3 - Gibraltar - 1:45 P.M.;
Desk 4 - Singapore - 12:30 P.M.;
Desk 5 - Lisbon - 2:00 P.M.

52

Ticket 008 wasn't pink (clue 1), yellow or white (clue 2), so green and (3) won a pen. Ticket 054 wasn't pink (1), or white (2), so yellow and Andrea had 008. Ticket 146 didn't win the clock (1), or the vase (4), so a cake. Wendy didn't win the cake (4), so Sharon who won the vase had ticket 054 and Wendy had ticket 100 and (by elimination) won the clock. Karen had ticket 146 (cake, above). Karen's ticket was pink (1), so Wendy's was white.

Thus:

Andrea - 008 - green - pen;
Karen - 146 - pink - cake;
Sharon - 054 - yellow - vase;
Wendy - 100 - white - clock.

53

The man whose birthday was on Monday isn't Don (clue 1), Ryan (clue 2), or Harry (3), so Mark. Either Don's birthday was on Wednesday and the man who received golf clubs had a birthday on Thursday (1), or Don's was on Thursday and the man who received golf clubs had a birthday on Friday. In other words,

Thursday's birthday was that of either Don or the man who received golf clubs. Thus Harry who received a telescope (3) didn't have a birthday on Thursday. Thursday's birthday wasn't Ryan's (2), so Don's, and the man who received golf clubs had a birthday on Friday. By elimination, he's Ryan and Harry's birthday was on Wednesday. Ryan isn't married to Olivia (1), Janet (2), or Claire (3), so Rose. Harry's wife isn't Janet (2), or Claire (3), so Olivia. Don's wife isn't Claire (3), so Janet who (2) gave the fishing rod. Mark thus received a camera from Claire.

Thus:

Don - Janet - fishing rod - Thursday;
Harry - Olivia - telescope - Wednesday;
Mark - Claire - camera - Monday;
Ryan - Rose - golf clubs - Friday.

54

Remember throughout that Tim went to two different places each day (intro). On the evening he went to the cinema, he hadn't spent the afternoon at the social club (clue 2), shops or library (clue 4), so the swimming pool. This wasn't on Thursday or Friday (3), Monday or Tuesday (4), so Wednesday. The evening trip to the shops was on Thursday (3). On the evening he went to the social club, he didn't go to the library or cinema in the afternoon (2), so the shops. His evening trip to the swimming pool was on Tuesday (4), so he spent Monday afternoon at the shops. By elimination Friday evening was spent at the library. He didn't go to the social club on Friday afternoon (2), so the cinema. He wasn't at the library on Thursday afternoon (1), so the social club. Tim's afternoon trip to the library was on Tuesday.

Thus (afternoon - evening):

Monday - shops - social club;
Tuesday - library - swimming pool;
Wednesday - swimming
    pool - cinema;
Thursday - social club - shops;
Friday - cinema - library.

55

The distance of 19 miles (shortest) wasn't covered on Thursday (clue 1), Monday (clue 2), Tuesday or Wednesday (4), so Friday. Thus they cycled 24 miles on Thursday (1), and 22 miles on the day they went to Big River. They cycled 22 miles on Tuesday (4), and 21 miles on Wednesday, so 25 miles on Monday to (1) Waterford. Wednesday's trip wasn't to Arkhill (2), so Rockfort (3), and they went to Edge Point on Thursday. Friday's trip was to Arkhill.

Thus:

Monday - 25 miles - Waterford;
Tuesday - 22 miles - Big River;
Wednesday - 21 miles - Rockfort;
Thursday - 24 miles - Edge Point;
Friday - 19 miles - Arkhill.

56

Geraldine's book is *Enigma* (clue 3), and Candice's is *Lost Cause* (clue 4). Angela is Dorothy's sister (2) whose book isn't *Sanctuary*, so *Water's Edge*. *Sanctuary* belongs to Fiona. The book to be read first isn't *Water's Edge* (1), *Sanctuary* (2), or *Enigma* (3), so *Lost Cause*. It belongs to her cousin (3), so *Water's Edge* won't be read second (1). Thus *Water's Edge* (which belongs to her sister, above) will be read third (2), and *Sanctuary* fourth. *Enigma* will be read second. *Sanctuary* doesn't belong to Dorothy's aunt (1), so her mother. *Enigma* belongs to her aunt.

Thus:

Enigma - Geraldine - Aunt - second;
Lost Cause - Candice - cousin - first;
Sanctuary - Fiona - mother - fourth;
Water's Edge - Angela - sister - third.

57

Harriet was Ivor's lover (clue 2), so Sheila was his wife. His business partner wasn't Vincent (clue 3), so Gary. Vincent was his cousin. Gary's motive was money (3), so Vincent was the *man* (1) whose motive was revenge. Harriet's motive wasn't blackmail (2), so jealousy. Sheila's motive was blackmail. The person who had known Ivor for 21 years wasn't Sheila (2), so Vincent hadn't known him for 16 or 21 years (1), and (3) Ivor hadn't known him for 21 years. Thus Harriet had known Ivor for 21 years. The person who had known him for 6 years wasn't Sheila (1), or Gary (3), so Vincent. Gary had known Ivor for 11 years (3), and Sheila for 16 years.

Thus:

Gary - business partner - money - 11 years;
Harriet - lover - jealousy - 21 years;
Sheila - wife - blackmail - 16 years;
Vincent - cousin - revenge - 6 years.

58

The person who arrived first wasn't Ian or Hans (clue 1), Rosie (clue 2), or Lola (3), so Sean. The second wasn't Ian (1), Rosie (2), or Lola (3), so Hans. Sean bought 10 stamps (1), so Hans bought 12 (2), and Rosie bought 13 (three more than Sean). Lola arrived later than Rosie (3), and Rosie arrived later than whoever bought 15 stamps (2). So Ian was third and bought 15, Rosie was fourth and Lola was fifth and bought 9 stamps.

Thus:

Hans - second - 12 stamps;
Ian - third - 15 stamps;
Lola - fifth - 9 stamps;
Rosie - fourth - 13 stamps;
Sean - first - 10 stamps.

59

The boots were bought on Tuesday (clue 2). Friday's purchase wasn't of the slippers (clue 1), sandals (3), or stilettos (4), so the trainers. They weren't from Heale's (4), so (1) the slippers were bought on Wednesday and the shoes from Heale's were bought on Thursday. They weren't stilettos (4), so sandals, and the stilettos were bought on Monday. Friday's purchase was from Cosy-Fit (3). The visit to Sharp's Shoes (1) wasn't on Wednesday (slippers, above), so (5) Wednesday's purchase was from Shoe Box and Tuesday's was from In-Step. Monday's was from Sharp's Shoes.

Thus:

Monday - stilettos - Sharp's Shoes;
Tuesday - boots - In-Step;
Wednesday - slippers - Shoe Box;
Thursday - sandals - Heale's;
Friday - trainers - Cosy-Fit.

60

The child who went on Monday isn't Ruth (clue 1), Patrick (clue 2), or Johnnie (4), so Mary. Ruth went on Thursday (1). The historical drama was seen on Tuesday (1). The comedy wasn't seen on Wednesday or Thursday (4), so Monday. Mary was taken by her uncle (4), so the aunt's treat was on Tuesday (2), and Patrick's was on Wednesday. Johnnie was thus taken by his aunt.

Ruth wasn't taken by a brother (3), so by her sister, and Patrick went with his brother. Ruth chose the western (4), so the sci-fi film was chosen by Patrick.

Thus:

Johnnie - Tuesday - aunt - historical;
Mary - Monday - uncle - comedy;
Patrick - Wednesday - brother - sci-fi;
Ruth - Thursday - sister - western.

61

Norma bought a poster for Zoë (clue 4), and the one of puppies was bought by Dave (clue 5). The tiger poster was bought for Carl, but not by Philip (3), so Cheryl. The poster for Marilyn cost either $4.20 or $4.50 (1), as did the poster for Neil (2), so Cheryl didn't pay $4.20 or $4.50. Thus Cheryl paid $4.80 (1), Marilyn's poster was $4.50, and Neil's was $4.20. By elimination, Zoë's poster cost $5.00. The poster of the hockey player cost $4.50 (2), so (by elimination) was bought by Philip. Thus the $4.20 poster was of puppies (2), and the $5.00 poster was of the pop star.

Thus (buyer - for):

$4.20 - Dave - Neil - puppies;
$4.50 - Philip - Marilyn -
      hockey player;
$4.80 - Cheryl - Carl - tiger;
$5.00 - Norma - Zoë - pop star.

62

No. 10 isn't directly opposite any other house (map). The boy at No. 10 isn't Ben or Max (clue 1), Derek (clue 2), or Timothy (3), so Ray. Thus Timothy lives at No. 9 (3). Max lives at No. 8 (1), the Wheeler boy at No. 9 and Ben at No. 7. Derek lives at No. 6. Max's surname is Myers (2), and Ben's is Dane. Ray's surname isn't Smith (3), so Clark. Derek's surname is Smith.

Thus:

No. 6 - Derek - Smith;
No. 7 - Ben - Dane;
No. 8 - Max - Myers;
No. 9 - Timothy - Wheeler;
No. 10 - Ray - Clark.

63

Remember throughout that each new picture contains pieces of three old ones (intro). The cat's body is with the duck's legs (clue 1), and the dog's head is with the horse's body (clue 2). Thus the tiger's head and dog's legs (3) are with the duck's body. The cat's body is thus with the horse's head, so (4) the cat's legs are with the duck's head. Thus the dog's head is with the tiger's legs and the cat's head is with the horse's legs. The dog's body isn't with the cat's legs (5), so the horse's legs. The duck's head is with the tiger's body.

SOLUTIONS

Thus (head - body - legs):
Cat - dog - horse;
Dog - horse - tiger;
Duck - tiger- cat;
Horse - cat - duck;
Tiger - duck - dog.

64

The 15-month-old dog's collar wasn't yellow (clue 1), green (clue 2), or blue (3), so red. The dog that finished first didn't wear the yellow collar (1), or blue collar (3), so the red collar (2), and the dog in the green collar was second. The dog in the yellow collar wasn't fourth (1), so third, and Zach was second. The dog in the blue collar was fourth. The 15-month-old dog (red collar, above) isn't Floss (2), so Floss is 17 months old and the dog in the green collar is 19 months old. The blue-collared dog is thus 18 months old. Bobby's collar isn't blue (3), so red. Misty's collar is blue.

Thus:
Bobby- 15 months old - red - first;
Floss - 17 months old - yellow - third;
Misty - 18 months old - blue - fourth;
Zach - 19 months old - green
   - second.

65

Cocktail D isn't the Sky High (clue 1), Kick Start (clue 2), or Lazy Slurp (3), so the Duck's Fizz. Cocktail A isn't the Sky High (1), or Lazy Slurp (3), so the Kick Start. It wasn't ordered by

Helen (1), Sarah (2), or Laura (3), so Brenda. Laura ordered the Lazy Slurp (3). The Sky High wasn't ordered by Helen (1), so Sarah. Helen ordered the Duck's Fizz. Cocktail A is Brenda's (above), so (3), Laura's is C and Sarah's is B. Sarah's is blue (2), so cocktail A is orange (1). Cocktail C isn't purple (4), so green. Cocktail D is purple.

Thus:
A - orange - Kick Start - Brenda;
B - blue - Sky High - Sarah;
C - green - Lazy Slurp - Laura;
D - purple - Duck's Fizz - Helen.

66

Oliver's surname is Blane (clue 4), so the boy surnamed Peters (3) who has chicken pox is Adam. The Jarvis child isn't Tina or Karen (1), so Joanna. Tina has the mumps (1), so the Wilder child with tonsillitis (2) is Karen. Tina's surname is Arden. Oliver hasn't influenza (4), so he has the measles and Joanna has influenza.

Thus:
Adam - Peters - chicken pox;
Joanna - Jarvis - influenza;
Karen - Wilder - tonsillitis;
Oliver - Blane - measles;
Tina - Arden - mumps.

67

The interviews on Monday and Tuesday weren't with Carlos Kato (clue 1), Jim O'Neill (clue 2), or Samuel Smith (3), so either Bella Jones and/or Paul Porter. Samuel Smith was in Peru (3). Neither Bella Jones nor Paul Porter was in Brazil (4). Monday's interview wasn't in Argentina (1), or Chile (3), so Ecuador. Tuesday's wasn't in Argentina (1), so Chile. Thus he met with Samuel Smith on Wednesday (3). Carlos Kato wasn't in Argentina (1), so Brazil, and Jim O'Neill was in Argentina. The interview with Carlos Kato wasn't on Friday (1), so Thursday, and that with Jim O'Neill was on Friday. Paul Porter was interviewed on Tuesday (1), so Bella Jones on Monday.

Thus:

Bella Jones - Ecuador - Monday;
Carlos Kato - Brazil - Thursday;
Jim O'Neill - Argentina - Friday;
Paul Porter - Chile - Tuesday;
Samuel Smith - Peru - Wednesday.

68

Felicity is on the *Ocean Winner* (clue 3). Richard is on the *Sea Sprite*, but not with Grace (clue 4), or Camilla (2), so Denise. Arthur's wife isn't Grace (2), or Felicity (6), so Camilla. Theirs is the diamond wedding anniversary (6). The

man on the *Ocean Breeze* who is celebrating his ruby wedding anniversary isn't Paul (5), so Terry. Thus Paul is on the *Ocean Winner* (with Felicity, 3), and Arthur is on the *Sea Queen*. By elimination, Terry's wife is Grace. Denise and (above) Richard aren't celebrating a silver wedding anniversary (1), so golden. Paul and Felicity are celebrating their silver wedding anniversary.

Thus:

Arthur - Camilla - diamond -
    Sea Queen;
Paul - Felicity - silver - *Ocean Winner*;
Richard - Denise - golden -
    Sea Sprite;
Terry - Grace - ruby - *Ocean Breeze*.

69

The blue sofa is either B or C (clue 1), as is the cream sofa (clue 3). Sofa D isn't green (4), so burgundy; thus A is green. D isn't priced at $229 (4), and hasn't a cotton cover (1), thus C isn't blue. No sofa is $209 (grid), so C isn't $229 (4). Thus B is blue, A is $229 (1), and C has a cotton cover and (by elimination) is cream. Either D is $159 and C is $179 (4), or D is $179 and C is $199. In other words, the $179 sofa is either C or D. So the $179 sofa is D (3), and B has chenille covers. C is $199 (4), so B is $159. The leather sofa isn't D (2), so A. The chintz is D.

Thus:

A - leather - green - $229;
B - chenille - blue - $159;
C - cotton - cream - $199;
D - chintz - burgundy - $179.

70

Graeme made either 9 or 10 calls on Christmas Eve (clue 4), and either 8 or 9 calls on Christmas Day. So he's not the person who made 9 calls on Christmas Eve (clue 1), and two fewer than Freda on Christmas Day. So Graeme made 10 calls on Christmas Eve. The person who made 6 on Christmas Day isn't Freda (1), Hal (2), or Iris (3), so Jimmy. The one who made 5 on Christmas Day isn't Freda (1), or Iris (3), so Hal. The person who made 7 on Christmas Day isn't Iris (3), so Freda. Hal made 9 on Christmas Eve (1). Jimmy made 7 on Christmas Eve (2), so Iris made 9 on Christmas Day (3), and Graeme made 8 on Christmas Day. Frieda didn't make 8 on Christmas Eve (4), so 6. Iris made 8 calls on Christmas Eve.

Thus (Eve - Day):

Freda - 6 calls - 7 calls;
Graeme - 10 calls - 8 calls;
Hal - 9 calls - 5 calls;
Iris - 8 calls - 9 calls;
Jimmy - 7 calls - 6 calls.

71

The man in cell 5 is serving either 20 or 22 years (clue 3), so (clue 2 and diagram) one of the men serving 15 or 25 years is in either cell 1 or cell 3. Thus neither is Sam White, who is in either cell 4 or cell 5. The man serving 15 years isn't John Fox (2), Phil Grant (3), or Roger Plum (4), so Dan Digby. Thus he's in either cell 2 or cell 3 and the man serving 22 years (1) is in cell 4 or cell 5. Thus Roger Plum isn't serving 25 years (4), so 18 years and Dan Digby is in cell 3. The man serving 25 years is in cell 2 (above), and the one serving 22 years is in cell 4 (1). The man in cell 5 is serving 20 years (3), so the man in cell 1 is serving 18 years. Sam White has cell 5 (5), and John Fox has cell 2, so Phil Grant has cell 4.

Thus:

Cell 1 - Roger Plum - 18 years;
Cell 2 - John Fox - 25 years;
Cell 3 - Dan Digby - 15 years;
Cell 4 - Phil Grant - 22 years;
Cell 5 - Sam White - 20 years.

72

Cathy met Pat at a party, and Naomi met him at a dance (clue 1). Bella met him on Thursday, but not at a nightclub (clue 3), so the swimming pool, where (2) she told him to "Take a dive!". Pat was told to "Get lost!" on Wednesday (2). Elaine told him to "Clear off!" on Friday (4), and the party was on Saturday. Thus Naomi met him on Wednesday and Friday's encounter was at a nightclub. Pat was told to "Shove off!" on Saturday.

Thus:

Wednesday - Naomi - dance - "Get lost!";

Thursday - Bella - swimming pool - "Take a dive!";

Friday - Elaine - nightclub - "Clear off!";

Saturday - Cathy - party - "Shove off!".

73

Darren is 9 (clue 2), so Anna is 8 (clue 3), and the child who provided items for the nose and eyes is 7. Darren's surname isn't Player (2), so the Player child is 10 (3). The child who provided the hat is thus 8 (1), and the Ford child is 9. Darren didn't provide the broom (2), so the scarf. Andrew's surname is Cliff (2), so Anna's is Marks and Donna's is Player. By elimination, Andrew is 7 years old.

Thus:

Andrew - Cliff - 7 - nose/eyes;

Anna - Marks - 8 - hat;

Darren - Ford - 9 - scarf;

Donna - Player - 10 - broom.

74

The 10:20 A.M. visit wasn't to the roses (clue 2), lavender (clue 3), mimosa or carnations (4), so jasmine and (1) the 10:15 A.M. move was due to noisy children. The 10:00 A.M. move wasn't due to rain (2), birds (3), or a cat (5), so no more nectar. Birds didn't cause the move at 10:20 A.M. (1), so 10:10 A.M. (3), and the lavender visit was at 10:00 A.M. The roses were visited at 10:15 A.M. (2), and rain caused the 10:20 A.M. move. Thus the move due to a cat was at 10:05 A.M. He visited the mimosa at 10:10 A.M. (4), and the carnations at 10:05 A.M.

Thus:

10:00 A.M. - lavender - no more nectar;

10:05 A.M. - carnations - cat;

10:10 A.M. - mimosa - birds;

10:15 A.M. - roses - children;

10:20 A.M. - jasmine - rain.

75

Monday's arrival with the damaged wing wasn't Delilah (clue 3), Samson (clue 2), Sheba, or Jezebel (4), so Solomon. The bird with an injured beak was brought in on Wednesday (2), so the one with a broken leg was brought in on Tuesday (4), Sheba on Wednesday, and Jezebel on Thursday. Samson was brought in on Friday (2), so Delilah on Tuesday. The swan with oil on its feathers arrived on Thursday

(1), and the one that swallowed a fish hook arrived on Friday.

Thus:

Delilah - broken leg - Tuesday;
Jezebel - oil on feathers - Thursday;
Samson - fish hook - Friday;
Sheba - injured beak - Wednesday;
Solomon - damaged wing - Monday.

76

The girl with a blue toothbrush has a pair of white pajamas (clue 4). The girl with an orange toothbrush has striped pajamas (clue 3), which aren't orange (intro), so blue or green, as is Dawn's toothbrush (3). Betty's pajamas are green (2), so her toothbrush isn't green (intro), thus it's either orange or white, as is Cara's (4). Anne's toothbrush is (by elimination) either blue or green, as are the pajamas with spots (1). The green pajamas haven't spots (2), so Anne's toothbrush is blue (1), and the blue pajamas have spots. By elimination, the striped pajamas are green, Dawn's toothbrush is green (3), and Cara's is white. The girl with blue pajamas isn't Dawn (3), so Cara. Dawn's pajamas haven't stars (3), so Anne's have stars and Dawn's have flowers and are orange.

Thus (toothbrush - pajamas):

Anne - blue - white - stars;
Betty - orange - green - stripes;
Cara - white - blue - spots;
Dawn - green - orange - flowers.

77

The man with the king of spades hasn't the ace or jack of hearts (clue 1), or the 4 of hearts (clue 3), so the man with the king of spades has the 7 of hearts. John has either the 2 or 3 of diamonds (2), but not the 7 of hearts. Thus John has the jack of hearts (2), the man with the 4 of hearts has the 7 of spades (3), and John has the 10 of spades. By elimination, the man with the ace of hearts has the 3 of spades. The man with the king of spades isn't Ian or Harry (1), so Kenny. Ian has the 4 of hearts (1), so Harry has the ace. Ian has the 2 of diamonds (4), so (above) John has the 3 of diamonds. Harry (ace of hearts, above) doesn't have the queen of diamonds (5), so the jack. Kenny has the queen of diamonds.

Thus (diamond - heart - spade):

Harry - J - A - 3;
Ian - 2 - 4 - 7;
John - 3 - J - 10;
Kenny - Q - 7 - K.

78

Friday's step class doesn't start at 10:30 A.M. or 11:00 A.M. (clue 3), so the yoga class (clue 2) is on Tuesday (2), and the 11:00 A.M. class is on Wednesday. Yoga starts at 10:30 A.M. (2), the trampoline class is at 2:30 P.M. (1), and Thursday's is at 11:30 A.M. Thus Friday's class is at 2:00 P.M., so Saturday's is at 2:30 P.M. The step class starts at 2:00 P.M. (3). The aerobics class isn't on Thursday (3), so Wednesday. The swimming class is on Thursday.

Thus:
Aerobics - 11:00 A.M. - Wednesday;
Step - 2:00 P.M. - Friday;
Swimming - 11:30 A.M. - Thursday;
Trampoline - 2:30 P.M. - Saturday;
Yoga - 10:30 A.M. - Tuesday.

79

Thomas is a driver today (clue 2), and David is a waiter today (clue 4). Gordon who is a cleaner (3) isn't today working as a postman (clue 1), so a porter. The man who is usually a porter is working as a postman today (1), thus he's either Kevin or Lou. Because Gordon is usually a cleaner and is working as a porter today (above), he isn't today doing the job Kevin would usually do (4). So the man whose usual job is that of porter isn't Kevin. Thus Lou is usually a porter and (1) is today working as a postman. By elimination, Kevin is working as a cleaner today. The man who is usually a waiter isn't Kevin (4), so Thomas. Thomas is working as a driver today, so (4) Kevin is usually a driver. By elimination, David usually works as a postman.

Thus (usual - today):
David - postman - waiter;
Gordon - cleaner - porter;
Kevin - driver - cleaner;
Lou - porter - postman;
Thomas - waiter - driver.

80

Brendan's friend lives 5 miles away (clue 3). The 4-mile trip wasn't for George (clue 2), or Colleen (3), so Marianne. The child who bought a comic on Saturday isn't Colleen or Brendan (3), or George (2), so Marianne. Thus George who bought a book (2) was collected on Friday. Brendan wasn't collected on Thursday (2), so Wednesday. Colleen was collected on Thursday. The 6-mile trip was on Friday (1), and candy was bought on Wednesday. Thursday's trip was 8 miles and involved lemonade.

Thus:
Wednesday - Brendan - 5 miles - candy;
Thursday - Colleen - 8 miles - lemonade;
Friday - George - 6 miles - book;
Saturday - Marianne - 4 miles - comic.

81

Remember throughout that each man exercised on three different days (intro). The man who swam on Monday isn't Stephan (clue 1), Bill (clue 2), or Frank (4), so Arthur. Bill swam on either Thursday or Friday (3), as did Frank (4), so Stephan swam on Tuesday. Arthur cycled on Friday or Saturday (2), so (1) Stephan cycled on Thursday or Friday. The man who cycled on Wednesday isn't Bill (4), so Frank. Bill didn't cycle on Saturday (4), so Arthur cycled on Saturday (1), and Stephan on Friday. Thus Bill cycled on Thursday, so he swam on Friday and Frank swam on Thursday. Stephan walked on Thursday (3), and Arthur on Wednesday (4). Since Bill swam on Friday (above) he walked on Tuesday and Frank walked on Friday.

Thus (cycled - swam - walked):
Arthur - Saturday - Monday - Wednesday;
Bill - Thursday - Friday - Tuesday;
Frank - Wednesday - Thursday - Friday;
Stephan - Friday - Tuesday - Thursday.

82

The sales starting at 8:30 A.M. and 10:00 A.M. aren't on Wednesday or Thursday (clue 1), or Friday (clue 4). The 10:00 A.M. sale isn't on Monday (2), so Tuesday and the 8:30 A.M. sale is on Monday. The toy shop sale starts at 9:30 A.M. (5), so Friday's sale at the book shop (4) starts at 9:00 A.M. The sale starting at 9:15 A.M. is the day after the shoe shop sale (6), so either the 9:15 A.M.

sale is on Wednesday and the shoe shop sale is Tuesday, or the 9:15 A.M. sale is on Thursday and the shoe shop sale is Wednesday. In other words, Wednesday's is either at 9:15 A.M. or at the shoe shop. Thus the 9:30 A.M. toy shop sale isn't on Wednesday, so Thursday. The 9:15 A.M. sale is thus on Wednesday (6), and the shoe shop sale is on Tuesday (10:00 A.M., above). The music shop sale doesn't start at 8:30 A.M. (3), so 9:15 A.M., and the clothing shop sale starts at 8:30 A.M.

Thus:
Book shop - Friday - 9:00 A.M.;
Clothing shop - Monday - 8:30 A.M.;
Music shop - Wednesday - 9:15 A.M.;
Shoe shop - Tuesday - 10:00 A.M.;
Toy shop - Thursday - 9:30 A.M.

83

No woman is giving 9 dolls (grid). The woman giving 7 isn't Harriet or Christine (clue 1), Danielle (clue 2), or Nicola (3), so Josie. Either Harriet is giving 8 and Christine is giving 10 (1), or Harriet is giving 10 and Christine is giving 12. In other words, the woman giving 10 is either Christine or Harriet, and (4) owns Tilly. Neither Nicola nor Josie owns Angelique or Serena (3), so their dolls are Bella and/or Jessica. Nicola is giving more dolls than a woman who isn't Josie (3), so Nicola isn't giving 8. Thus Nicola is giving 11 (3), and the woman keeping Angelique is giving 12. Harriet's doll isn't Serena (1), so Tilly (giving 10, above). Thus Christine is giving 12 (1), so Danielle is giving 8. By elimination, Danielle's doll is Serena. Josie's is Bella (2), so Nicola's is Jessica.

Thus:

Christine - 12 dolls - Angelique;
Danielle - 8 dolls - Serena;
Harriet - 10 dolls - Tilly;
Josie - 7 dolls - Bella;
Nicola - 11 dolls - Jessica.

84

The man who stayed on for 35 seconds isn't 22 (clue 2), 25 (clue 3), or 18 (4), so 20. He isn't Danny (1), Joe (4), or Chuck (6), so Scott. Scott isn't A or B (4), or D (6), so C, and the man who stayed on for 55 seconds is B or D (5). B is 25 (3). D isn't 22 (2), so 28. A is 22. The man who stayed on for 55 seconds thus isn't D (1), so B. A stayed on for 48 seconds and Joe for 41 seconds (4), so Joe is D. Chuck isn't 25 (3), so 22. Danny is 25.

Thus:

Rider A - Chuck - 22 - 48 seconds;
Rider B - Danny - 25 - 55 seconds;
Rider C - Scott - 20 - 35 seconds;
Rider D - Joe - 28 - 41 seconds.

85

Remember throughout that the three forenames and the surname of each family start with four different letters (intro). Miss Mitchell's father isn't Mike or Robert (clue 1), and her mother isn't Mandy or Rosemary. Thus her parents' names begin with P or S, so Miss Mitchell isn't Priscilla or Susan, thus she's Rachel. Her mother isn't Patricia (clue 3), so Sally, and her father is thus Peter. Robert's surname is Sanders (1), so (by elimination) Rosemary's surname is Pringle, Priscilla's mother is Mandy and Mike's daughter is Susan. Susan's surname isn't Pringle (2), so Rothman. Thus Moira's surname is Pringle and Priscilla's is Sanders. Saul's surname is Pringle and Patricia's is Rothman.

Thus (husband - wife - daughter):

Mitchell - Peter - Sally - Rachel;
Pringle - Saul - Rosemary - Moira;
Rothman - Mike - Patricia - Susan;
Sanders - Robert - Mandy - Priscilla.

86

Remember throughout that each new picture contains pieces of three old ones (intro). Norma's grandpa's body is with her uncle's legs (clue 2), so her cousin's head (clue 4) is with her uncle's body. Her grandpa's head is with her sister's body (1), and her grandpa's legs are with her aunt's head (3). By elimination, her aunt's head is with her cousin's body, her

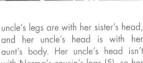
uncle's legs are with her sister's head, and her uncle's head is with her aunt's body. Her uncle's head isn't with Norma's cousin's legs (5), so her sister's legs. Thus her cousin's head is with her aunt's legs and her grandpa's head is with her cousin's legs.

Thus (head - body - legs):
Aunt - cousin - grandpa;
Cousin - uncle - aunt;
Grandpa - sister - cousin;
Sister - grandpa - uncle;
Uncle - aunt - sister.

87

The person who ironed 10 items isn't Wendy (clue 2), Margaret (clue 3), Brian (4), or Alison (5), so Simon, and (1) Wendy ironed 11 items. No one ironed 12 items (grid), so (4) Brian ironed one more item than (by elimination) Margaret, who did the ironing the day after Alison. Alison didn't iron 15 items (3), so Brian ironed 15, Margaret 14, and Alison 13. Wendy ironed earlier than Simon (2), so she ironed on Tuesday (5). Simon ironed two days after Margaret (3), and Margaret ironed the day after Alison (4), so Alison ironed on Wednesday, Margaret on Thursday and Simon on Saturday. Brian ironed on Friday.

Thus:
Alison - Wednesday - 13 items;
Brian - Friday - 15 items;
Margaret - Thursday - 14 items;
Simon - Saturday - 10 items;
Wendy - Tuesday - 11 items.

88

Coin C hasn't a value of 50 Fortunas (clue 2), or 10 Fortunas (clue 4). If its value is 5 Fortunas, then the value of B would be 20 Fortunas (3), and clue 5 cannot work. Thus C has a value of 20 Fortunas. B was found at the Temple of Athena (5), and A in 1933. D is the 5 Fortunas coin (5). C was found in 1919 (3), and A has a value of 10 Fortunas (4), so B's value is 50 Fortunas. D was found near the Temple of Artemis (2), and C was at the Temple of Zeus (1), so A was at the Temple of Hera. The 1951 find is D (4), so B was found in 1972.

Thus:
A - 10 Fortunas - 1933 - Hera;
B - 50 Fortunas - 1972 - Athena;
C - 20 Fortunas - 1919 - Zeus;
D - 5 Fortunas - 1951 - Artemis.

89

Remember throughout that each person visited three different towns (intro). The one who went to Whitby on Monday, Newcastle on Wednesday, and Ajax on Friday (clue 4) isn't Roger (who went to Kingston, clue 1), Kate (2), or Penny (3), so Adam. Penny went to Newcastle on Friday (3). Monday's trip to Newcastle wasn't made by Roger (5), so Kate. The *woman* who went to Kingston on Wednesday also went to Ajax (1), so she isn't Kate. Thus Penny went to Kingston on Wednesday (1), so on Monday she went to Ajax and Roger went to Kingston. Roger's Friday trip was to Whitby, so he went to Ajax on Wednesday. Kate went to Whitby on Wednesday and Kingston on Friday.

Thus (Mon - Wed - Fri):
Adam - Whitby - Newcastle - Ajax;
Kate - Newcastle - Whitby - Kingston;
Penny - Ajax - Kingston - Newcastle;
Roger - Kingston - Ajax - Whitby.

90

David's old number was either 73 or 81 (clue 2), and Nicholas's new number is either 66 or 74. Thus Edith's new number is 74 (clue 3), and her old one was 81. Thus Nicholas's new number is 66 (above), and (2) David's old number was 73. The person whose new number is 99 isn't Steve or Pamela (1), so David. Steve's old number wasn't 22 (1). If it was 31, then (1) his new number is 29, leaving no two numbers with a difference of seven for Pamela. So Steve's old number wasn't 31; thus it was 54. His new number isn't 38 (4),

so 29. Pamela's is thus 38, so her old number was 31 (1), and Nicholas's old number was 22.

Thus (old - new):
David - 73 - 99;
Edith - 81 - 74;
Nicholas - 22 - 66;
Pamela - 31 - 38;
Steve - 54 - 29.

91

The boy who spent 50 minutes in the pool isn't Charlie or Liam (clue 1), Graham (clue 3), or Ian (4), so Alan. Charlie was in the pool for 45 minutes (1), and Graham for 35 minutes (3). Charlie didn't swim 3 lengths (1). The boy who swam 4 lengths isn't Charlie or Alan (2). Charlie was in the pool for ten minutes longer than Graham (3), so (2) Graham didn't swim 4 lengths. Graham (35 minutes, above) didn't swim 3 lengths (2), so Ian didn't swim 4 lengths (4). Thus Liam swam 4 lengths. Charlie swam 6 lengths (1), so Graham swam 2 (4), and Ian swam 3 lengths. Alan swam 5 lengths. Ian was in the pool for 40 minutes (2), and Liam for 30 minutes.

Thus:
Alan - 50 minutes - 5 lengths;
Charlie - 45 minutes - 6 lengths;
Graham - 35 minutes - 2 lengths;
Ian - 40 minutes - 3 lengths;
Liam - 30 minutes - 4 lengths.

92

Victor doesn't excel in art or history (clue 1). So in clue 1, he's boy A; and in clue 2, he's the boy with a mark 4 percent lower than Chris's. Victor's mark wasn't 90% (clue 3), so 88% and Chris got 92% (2). The boy who got 90% (2 percent more than Victor) isn't Jake (1), so Neil. Thus Jake got 94%. In clue 1, Chris is the boy who excels at art, so he's boy C. Victor's subject isn't geography (3), so science. Neil's subject (90%, above) isn't geography (3), so history and Jake's is geography. Neil isn't boy B (2), so he's boy D and Jake is boy B.

Thus:

Boy A - Victor - science - 88%;
Boy B - Jake - geography - 94%;
Boy C - Chris - art - 92%;
Boy D - Neil - history - 90%.

93

Remember throughout that each basket contained three different quantities (intro). The basket with 5 bananas didn't have 4 apples (clue 1), so either 2 or 3 and the basket with 6 bananas had either 3 or 4 apples. In other words, the basket with 3 apples had either 5 or 6 bananas. The basket with 5 apples hadn't 4 bananas (clue 4), so 3 bananas. By elimination, the basket with 4 apples had 6 bananas, so the one with 3 apples had 5 bananas (1), and the one with 2 apples had 4 bananas.

Basket D didn't have 5 or 6 bananas (3). Since C's oranges numbered one more than D's bananas, C didn't have 4 apples (1), so didn't have 6 bananas (above). The basket with 6 bananas wasn't B (1), so A. B had 3 oranges (2), so A had 5 oranges (1), and the basket with 3 apples had 4 oranges. C had 4 oranges (3), and D had 3 bananas, plus 2 oranges. B had 2 apples and C had 3 apples.

Thus:

Basket A - 4 apples - 6 bananas - 5 oranges;
Basket B - 2 apples - 4 bananas - 3 oranges;
Basket C - 3 apples - 5 bananas - 4 oranges;
Basket D - 5 apples - 3 bananas - 2 oranges.

94

The woman who has sold 52 tickets isn't Leanne (clue 1), Denise (clue 2), or Sally (4). The one who has sold 55 tickets isn't Leanne (1), Bridget (2), or Sally (4). Thus the women who have sold 52 and 55 tickets are Amanda, Bridget, and/or Sally. If Amanda has sold 52, then Denise hasn't sold 55 (2), leaving no possibility for anyone to have sold 55 tickets. Bridget has sold 52 (2), and Denise has sold 55 tickets. The woman who has sold 35 isn't Leanne (1), or Amanda (3), so Sally. Amanda has sold 45 (3), and Leanne 38. Amanda is the cook (1), so

(4) Denise is the physician. Bridget is the midwife (1). The nurse isn't Leanne (3), so Sally. Leanne is the cleaner.

Thus:

Amanda - cook - 45 tickets;
Bridget - midwife - 52 tickets;
Denise - physician - 55 tickets;
Leanne - cleaner - 38 tickets;
Sally - nurse - 35 tickets.

95

Pot B has a pattern of diamonds (clue 3), so the pot with a zigzag pattern is D (clue 2), and the $61.00 pot is either A, B, or C. No pot costs $59.50 (grid). The pot costing $60.50 hasn't a design of diamonds or squares (3), or stars (4), so has either a floral pattern or a zigzag pattern (D, above). Pot A hasn't a floral pattern (1), so the $60.50 pot isn't A, thus the floral pattern isn't priced at $61.00. The $61.00 pot hasn't squares (3), or stars (4), so diamonds. Thus the pot with squares is $60.00. Pot C is $60.50 (4), and the pot with stars is $58.50. By elimination, C has a floral design and the zigzag pot costs $59.00. Pot A is (1) $60.00 (squares, above), so E has a design of stars.

Thus:

Pot A - squares - $60.00;
Pot B - diamonds - $61.00;
Pot C - floral - $60.50;
Pot D - zigzag - $59.00;
Pot E - star - $58.50.

96

The rooms seen at 2:00 P.M. aren't in Keats Court (clue 3), Milton Place, or Shelley Avenue (clue 4), so Byron Drive. Those costing $200 aren't in Keats Court (3), Milton Place, or Shelley Avenue (4), so Byron Drive. The rooms seen at 3:00 P.M. aren't $350 (1), or $300 (2), so $250. The travel time from the $300 rooms isn't 20 minutes (2), and that from the $250 rooms isn't 30 minutes (3), so the travel time from the $250 rooms is 20 minutes (1), and that from the $300 rooms is 15 minutes. The $300 rooms were seen at 5:00 P.M. (2), so the $350 rooms were seen at 4:00 P.M. The travel time from the $200 rooms isn't 30 minutes (3), so 25 and it would take 30 minutes from the $350 rooms. The Keats Court rooms weren't seen at 3:00 P.M. (1), or 4:00 P.M. (3), so 5:00 P.M. The Milton Place rooms were seen at 3:00 P.M. (4), and the Shelley Avenue rooms at 4:00 P.M.

Thus:

Byron Drive - 2:00 P.M. - $200 - 25 minutes;
Keats Court - 5:00 P.M. - $300 - 15 minutes;
Milton Place - 3:00 P.M. - $250 - 20 minutes;
Shelley Avenue - 4:00 P.M. - $350 - 30 minutes.

97

Remember throughout that each woman ate three different fruits and none ate the same fruit in the same order as anyone else (intro). Claire didn't eat an apple (clue 2), so her three fruits were (in some order) a banana, an orange, and a pear. Thus Claire didn't eat an orange third (clue 1), or second (3), so first; and (2) Teresa ate a banana second. Claire's second fruit was (by elimination) a pear, so her third was a banana. The woman who ate a banana first didn't eat an orange second (3), so she ate an apple second. By elimination, the woman who ate an apple third had a pear first, and the woman who ate an orange third (1) had an apple second. Thus the woman who ate an apple first had a pear third; so she isn't Stephanie (4). The woman who ate an apple first isn't Laura (4), so Teresa. Stephanie ate a pear (4), so (by elimination) she ate a pear first (and an apple third, above). Laura ate a banana first. Stephanie ate an orange second.

Thus (first - second - third):
Claire - orange - pear - banana;
Laura - banana - apple - orange;
Stephanie - pear - orange - apple;
Teresa - apple - banana - pear.

98

Of the five people in clue 2, Pauline isn't in seat A, so Samuel who is anticlockwise of Pauline isn't in seat E; and Samuel isn't in seat C, so Pauline isn't in D and the history student isn't in E. Thus in clue 2, the person in seat E is Pauline, the history student is in A, and Samuel is in D. Martine is one place clockwise of the chemistry student (1), so Martine isn't in B. Cathy is one place clockwise of Martine (1), so (since Pauline is in E, above), Cathy isn't in A. Thus Cathy is in B (1), the geography student is in C, the chemistry student is in E, and Martine is in A. By elimination, David is in C. Cathy's subject isn't biology (1), so mathematics. Samuel is the biology student.

Thus:
Seat A - Martine - history;
Seat B - Cathy - mathematics;
Seat C - David - geography;
Seat D - Samuel - biology;
Seat E - Pauline - chemistry.

99

Remember throughout the dates on the grid, and that no executive went to the same state in the same month as any other executive (intro). Each person spent a month in Alaska and a month in Florida (intro), so whoever went to Alaska in March didn't also go to Florida in March, and whoever went to Alaska in September didn't also go to Florida in September. September's trip to Alaska wasn't made by Tony (clue 2). No one went to Florida in July, so Peter didn't go to Alaska in September (clue 3). Nor was September's trip to Alaska made by Alice (4), or Naomi (5), so Michael went to Alaska in September. September's trip to Florida wasn't made by Peter (3), Alice (4), or Naomi (5), so by Tony. Peter went to Alaska in July (3). No one went to Alaska in February or June, so Alice didn't go to Alaska in April (1), thus Alice went to Alaska in either January or March, as did the person who went to Florida in May. By elimination, Tony went to Alaska in April, and Naomi went to Florida in May. Thus Naomi went to Alaska in January (5). So Peter went to Florida in March (2). Alice went to Alaska in March. She didn't go to Florida in August (3), so Michael went to Florida in August, and Alice went to Florida in February.

Thus (Alaska - Florida):
Alice - March - February;
Michael - September - August;
Naomi - January - May;
Peter - July - March;
Tony - April - September.

100

The avatar of the cook is a model (clue 2), and the virtual spy is called Francine. Thus the avatar known as Amanda who is a teacher by day (clue 4), but not a beautician when online, is a dealer when online. Anne is a driver by day (3). Her avatar's name isn't Amanda, Francine, or Melissa (3), so Stella; and Sue's avatar is Melissa. By elimination, the nurse calls herself Francine when online, and Anne plays the role of beautician in the virtual world. Molly's avatar is Francine (1), and Freda plays the role of a dealer. Sue is thus the cook.

Thus (Player - Player's job - Avatar - Avatar's job):
Anne - driver - Stella - beautician;
Freda - teacher - Amanda - dealer;
Molly - nurse - Francine - spy;
Sue - cook - Melissa - model.

COLLECT ALL TITLES IN
THE POCKET POSH® PUZZLE SERIES!